Spirit Told Me &
Synchronicity
Led the Way

❧ *A True Story* ❧

Alison Lakes

BALBOA.
PRESS

A DIVISION OF HAY HOUSE

Balboa Press books may be ordered through booksellers or by contacting:

Balboa Press
A Division of Hay House
1663 Liberty Drive
Bloomington, IN 47403
www.balboapress.com.au
1 (877) 407-4847

Because of the dynamic nature of the Internet, any web addresses or
links contained in this book may have changed since publication and may
no longer be valid. The views expressed in this work are solely those
of the author and do not necessarily reflect the views of the publisher,
and the publisher hereby disclaims any responsibility for them.

The author of this book does not dispense medical advice or prescribe the use
of any technique as a form of treatment for physical, emotional, or medical
problems without the advice of a physician, either directly or indirectly. The
intent of the author is only to offer information of a general nature to help
you in your quest for emotional and spiritual well-being. In the event you use
any of the information in this book for yourself, which is your constitutional
right, the author and the publisher assume no responsibility for your actions.

Any people depicted in stock imagery provided by Thinkstock are models,
and such images are being used for illustrative purposes only.
Certain stock imagery © Thinkstock.

Print information available on the last page.

ISBN: 978-1-4525-3052-9 (sc)
ISBN: 978-1-4525-3053-6 (e)

Balboa Press rev. date: 09/07/2015

CONTENTS

FOREWORD

In June 2014, I was living in Deception Bay, Queensland. One day I had to go to Brisbane on business, and I decided the train would be the best way to get there. The nearest station was Dakabin. I selected the train I needed to catch in order to get to my appointment on time.

As it turned out, I inadvertently caught an earlier train that happened to pull into the station shortly after my arrival—serendipity. As I entered the carriage, I noted that it was fairly full, with a few scattered seats still available.

Over the years, when I enter a room that is crowded, it has been my practice to pray and ask for guidance as to where or with whom I should sit. Invariably, I have been led to people whom I had not previously met face-to-face, but who—unknown to me—would become, or who already had been, an integral part of my life. Such has been the nature of my guidance.

So on this occasion, I again prayed and was directed to sit next to a well-dressed, well-presented middle-aged lady. Without any shyness we introduced ourselves, and I discovered that this very nice lady's name was Alison. It was not long before we were sharing our thoughts on spirituality and the paranormal.

Something about Alison reminded me of the famous English medium Rosemary Brown, who once talked with some very famous deceased composers and wrote down music that they "dictated" to her. I have read both her books, *Unfinished Symphonies: Voices from the Beyond* and *Immortals at My Elbow*. I watched her on television as she "received" music from Chopin, which was immediately authenticated by a world-famous pianist who was also present. I met and spoke with renowned concert pianist John Lill about Rosemary, knowing he had contributed a chapter to her book confirming some circumstances that involved Beethoven.

I mention Rosemary Brown because, like Alison, she had a demeanour that was quietly spoken and unassuming, which, to me, is the hallmark of a genuine psychic. Psychic gifts are sacred trusts, and only those who are genuine receive any respect from me. I had no doubts about Alison.

I have had many experiences, as Alison has, but obviously our life paths are uniquely different. I have met people in dreams whom I did not know but found out later were real live people. I have seen some people who, I subsequently found out, had actually passed on—once on the first anniversary of that person's demise, and on another occasion at the time of transition.

Alison mentioned the book she had been writing and that she needed a preliminary edit so that her manuscript would be on its way to being an acceptable standard to send to publishers. The editing would be time-consuming and, therefore, expensive, so I offered to assist her in this regard, which Alison accepted.

During the course of the subsequent editing, I was constantly aware of becoming more and more involved in the emotion of Alison's experiences, and at times I felt exhausted as I lived through them. I have endeavoured to preserve the integrity of Alison's story, which I hope will be a profound lesson for all those who are confused by the source of their own emotions and behaviours.

Alison's journey has been one of courage and determination—supported, thankfully, by the many intermittent, independent confirmations of her insightfulness.

Alison and I agreed that we had not had previous encounters in former lives, but I had not considered any encounters with connections in this life. When I shared the details of Alison's book with Grace, my previous wife, she announced that her ancestors had come from Culloden—a fact about which I had been completely unaware. Serendipity?

Fred Appleton
Composer, author, theatrical producer

ACKNOWLEDGEMENTS

My thanks to my most loyal and trusted friends—Amanda, Diane, and Lizzie. Without their support and understanding, there were times when I would have felt there was no point in going on. The only thing that kept me going was the minute possibility of seeing Stephen again. Although I had a dream of this taking place, it has not happened. Dreams can be driven by fear, hope, or portent.

To my travel mate Mary, whom I first met when I got to London, I would like to say that I appreciate the fact that you didn't ask too many questions. I found it hard to understand myself. I did not want to upset any religious beliefs you may hold. We got on so well, and I look forward to catching up for a visit when we can. I hope this book explains it all to you, my good friend.

To my friends Susan and Andrew—you helped me so much with the computer, for hours on end. Without your help, I doubt I would have stayed sane. Thank you.

Most of the characters' names have been changed to protect certain people.

While I can't prove that the visions described here actually occurred, most other things can easily be proved. There were so many who witnessed various events—thank goodness I kept a diary of both trips to help me remember them. I can only come to the conclusion that these were karmic events, which it seems I had to experience. However, they are experiences that, rest assured, I don't care to ever relive.

Alone Again

It was the start of a new life, and I was alone and single—but more than ready to start life again. Although my daughter initially lived with me, she quickly decided to join her boyfriend to make marriage plans, so I was really left on my own. I was living in beautiful Queensland Australia where the motto is "beautiful on day, perfect the next"

I had to borrow my daughter's car to move much of my stuff so there were many trips back and forwards from my previous home to my new place.

My motto at that time and even still today is "I haven't come this far to go backwards now" so even though there was a lot of stress and hard work, I kept going on.

Now living on my own was quite a different story and a new experience as I haven't been single since I was eighteen and a half. Getting married at that age was quite normal in those days.

Now I had other things to have to consider .Firstly shopping; having no car meant I had to walk everywhere. Luckily the shopping centre was only a ten minute walk away so I had to just buy the things I needed at the time and carry them in bags.

Some years ago I had hurt my back permanently while playing hockey which left me with constant pain. Numbness and pins and needles were my constant companion. Standing for any long period also gave me backache. My answer to this was to start walking in a serious way. Each morning at about 5am I would start the walk. I lived quite close to a major horse racing track where I could watch the beautiful racing horses get groomed and trained and go for the training runs. When they were washed, their skins were shining. Sometimes the jockey would walk them past me. The horses were quite tall which made the jockey seem even smaller than usual. There was so much activity going on before race days. Over a long time the benefit of walking did start to make a difference slowly, very slowly.

Not having a car meant walking everywhere. Sometimes a bike is not enough. If I needed to get into town, at least there was a bus stop across the road but many times I would walk home which took me about forty five minutes. Just to save some money. Halfway on my walk home I would walk through the city gardens which were beautiful. I could stop and smell the flowers and admire all the great work the council would do. It seemed to give me the extra energy to continue my walk home.

If I wanted any company, then my friends would have to come and see me at my place. I wouldn't allow myself to think about any problems that might come up as that might tend to get me down a bit and my health was not good enough as it was. It would take a long time to get my nerves settled, and find peace again. I didn't think of being lonely at night as the constant walking was making me tired enough to sleep. My other two sons lived a long way away so there was little they could help me with. There was no men around the flats to help me with any real problems that might require a man's expertise so again I just decided that there were not going to be any problems

A few months earlier, I'd had many dreams showing me how my life would work out, so I was not worried about the future.

I've kept a dream journal for more than twenty-five years, and it has been my practice to meticulously write down the details of my dreams, always recording the date as well. But, unfortunately, as a consequence of moving house a few times, I lost some of these records. Even so, thankfully, I still have many years of my journals saved.

Starting Over

I slipped the key into the lock of my newly rented flat, opened the door, and walked inside, feeling the silence all around me. I recall that it felt good.

I threw my keys onto the coffee table and looked around. I didn't have much furniture in the room; in addition to the coffee table, I had a twelve-inch television that belonged to my daughter, a small tape recorder for music, and a little three-piece cane lounge setting. However, the empty spaces didn't seem to matter.

I visited a second-hand store and purchased a fridge, a washing machine, a dining table and chairs, and a bed. I had all the essentials I needed, and I considered myself lucky. I did a little dance around the coffee table. I didn't know what was ahead of me, but I wasn't worried; I just felt like a kid again. I had my bike to get around, and I was good at managing my money, so I knew that financially, at least, there wouldn't be a problem.

My trust in men at that stage was non-existent, but that suited me just fine.

The home I had previously owned was on the market. I did miss the tropical gardens I had tended and the beautiful flowers at the front of the house. However, I was consoled by the thought that the next owner would appreciate them. Anyway, it was just practise for the next house. Being a gardener, I knew there would always be another garden.

At the rear of my flat, the owner hadn't made the grounds very presentable, so I asked if I could undertake that task. It wasn't long before I was growing some pretty flowers, making the small area lovely and colourful.

On reflection, considering my changed circumstances, I still had some good friends, and I had my sister. Happily, I was soon to find and join a church of spiritual seekers, where I found many more like-minded people. I had always heard that meditation was good for you, so I thought I would give it a go. I had such a busy mind that it took me about six weeks to get myself sufficiently quieted down to try it.

I had met Diane through the church and soon learnt of a meditation circle she held at her home. At that stage, I had no car, so Harry, another friend through the church, picked me up.

Diane was renting a big house on a property on the outskirts of town, which was divided into two flats, one for herself and the other for Harry. The flats were connected by a long hall, and it worked well for them.

Usually, there were between six and twelve people in the circle, so I soon got to know everyone. After an opening prayer, we would settle down to meditate. I really began to understand what people meant about the value of meditation. It was calming and sometimes fun, too, because as we went around the circle of people, each of us would tell the others if they'd picked up anything that they wished to share. I usually had, and I soon needed a pen and paper to remember everything.

This quickly became the best part of the night for me, and I was constantly amazed at the accurate and amusing things I would receive. This usually left me on a high for the rest of the night, and I couldn't get to sleep for hours afterwards.

It's hard to explain to others who do not understand how this happens, but I would see very clear pictures, and often I couldn't understand how these occurred. But I was always amazed at the information I received. Sometimes words would come out of my mouth before I realised I had spoken, surprising me.

In the past, I had been sceptical of such claims by others; however, after experiencing so many visualisations myself, I had to believe them. I just went along with what I received without question. Anyway, people would soon tell me if it was right or wrong.

The old saying is very true: never judge a person or think you can understand another's life or experiences until you've walked a mile in that person's shoes, and you are going to walk with me in this book in my shoes. Many times over the years, I had readings with clairvoyants, and I was consistently asked, "Why are you not doing this work yourself?"

I would always reply, "I don't have enough confidence." However, if I did get some visualisation that I strongly believed others needed to know, I usually would tell them anyway.

At times in the group, I would pick up information that made no sense to me at all. Even so, it usually meant something to one of the others. An incident occurred concerning a couple who were new to the group. When I contemplated the man, I picked up *heart problems*, but when I suggested this to him he said, "Not really," so I didn't pursue the matter.

I then turned to his wife and saw a picture of heaps of jelly beans, all different colours, so I asked, "Do you both like sweets?"

She said, "No, but my husband has diabetes and needs jelly beans in case his sugar levels go too low."

I then suggested that her husband would certainly be more likely to have heart problems if he had diabetes, and she agreed. So you see, dear reader, it usually makes sense to someone.

One night, when scanning one of the regular attendees, a man, I twice received big letters of warning saying *health*, so I asked him if he had some problem with his health. He replied no. Though I felt unsure about his answer, I did not pursue it; obviously, I couldn't argue with him, although something still prompted me to mention that a simple blood test could determine if he had diabetes. Not being a doctor, I didn't want to seem arrogant, so I let it go.

The following week, I got the same nudge again. I asked him about it once more, and again he replied no. So I didn't pursue it. The man didn't come back to the group for a few weeks. When he did, he announced that he had been diagnosed as having full-blown diabetes. Diane mentioned to him that someone had foretold this, and it was then that he remembered what I had told him.

On another occasion, there were two new women. As I concentrated on one of them, I got a picture of an old post-and-rail fence and a duck. It didn't make any sense to me, so I asked her if she lived on a farm or something. She laughed and said no, but on their way that night, they'd crossed an old bridge with old posts, and they'd had to stop the car in the middle of the bridge as a lone duck wandered across the road.

Next at Diane's meeting came my first real experience as a medium. At the outset, I sensed this was going to be different from my usual experience and mentioned this before I started sharing the information I was receiving.

In this first experience, I saw a pretty young girl about four or five years of age. She was speaking to me and telling me to say, "Tell them I can swim now." She seemed pretty happy about the idea. Sadly, I felt this young one had drowned and also that the event occurred not in an ocean but in still water surrounded by lots of greenery.

Diane claimed this connection. She said a relative of hers had lost a little girl many years ago, and it was by drowning in still water. Diane felt that the green landscape was because the event had occurred in the United Kingdom. She said she would try to find out more details, but after some weeks of enquiries, she found that the people connected to the event had passed away, so there was not much more she could determine.

Another two who joined meditation circle on the same night were an older woman and a younger man. Every time I concentrated on one, I got an image of the other. So I asked the younger man, not having been personally introduced, if somehow they were related, and he told me that they were mother and son. I asked further about a man "who was the grease monkey," as I could see a man underneath a car. He confirmed he had planned to do work on a car.

Then I was prompted to ask if there was a birthday or something coming up, because I could see a cake to celebrate a special occasion, and they advised that there was one planned.

One important image occurred while in meditation. I saw our group as a small candle-like globe. Then the picture expanded, as if the whole world had shrunk before me into a small ball, and I saw lots of globe-like lights similar to our group all around that image of the world. I interpreted this as showing me that there were many other groups around the globe trying to make a difference by making the world a better place.

It's a pity that the phenomenon of the many groups with similar aspirations does not get any publicity. Unfortunately, bad behaviour gets all the media attention, when in reality, so many people are trying to better the world in their own small way.

Reincarnation

I find the idea of reincarnation to be much more acceptable today, especially with some genuinely talented mediums around. I think it is of great benefit to those who get confirmation from loved ones on the other side, who give details that only the people concerned can verify. You can see how such public performances sell out so quickly now that there is so much interest in this phenomenon.

When I first heard the word *reincarnation* explained, it just felt right to me, and the more I learnt, the more it made sense. After all, if, as is postulated, we choose the life and circumstances we are going to be born into, then we've done so for a reason.

Usually, as put forward by those who subscribe to this understanding, we are here to learn lessons we've avoided, to right a wrong, or to just be better people or advance our spiritually. It is suggested that many come with a definite mission and know that they are here to make the world a better place—these are said to include Princess Diana, Steve Irwin, John Denver, Martin Luther King, and Mother Teresa, among others. It's a bit like being in a play at school where we play a part for a while. We might choose the part we want to play, but when it's finished, we just walk off the stage to resume our life.

I do not believe that we can dismiss the many thousands of people from all countries, over many centuries and different cultures, who have believed in reincarnation by suggesting that they are wrong. This belief has been passed down over many generations and is much more accepted today as more and more evidence is provided by so many, including medical practitioners and children.

It makes no sense to me that some people are born into riches while others are born into poverty. It seems so unfair. If we just die at the end, and finish up as ashes or in a box, what is it all for? What have we gained? And of what use is it? Is it just bad luck? What is the point?

I look at it like this: When we are young, we start school at the age of about five years old. If we finish the year and do well we go on to another level above that, and so on, year after year. If we fail one year, often we have to repeat that year before we can progress further. So we keep on, as if we are going through to high school and then on to higher education. From there we think about our employment, and in what area we would like to participate, and so there is more learning. Sometimes we decide we are on a wrong course and change tack by taking up a different area of study, all the while getting more experience from the unlimited options that are available to us in this life.

So think of the same process, but this time the years of school are our different lives. We continue to learn more from each life. When we're young, we think we know it all at each of the different stages, but in reality, with the advantage of hindsight, we see that we knew very little. Something that we only realise as we get older is that we still have so much to learn but so little time left in which to do it.

If we are going through a bad time, we may well ask, "Why should we choose this process to go through? It's so awful!" I also asked this question many times when I was younger. It's a big hurdle to overcome, but after much deep thinking and a lack of any other explanation, I could come to no other conclusion than to see the hard times as lessons. Life is not what we have to deal with, but rather how we handle it. We often don't realise this until we have some wisdom behind us. I wish that I'd known this at a time when I could see no light at the end of the tunnel—when I was young and desperate. I wish I'd had someone explain this to me and use it to help me through the bad times.

I would add here that at one stage, I did read the Bible right through, but it gave me more questions than answers. Also, we must acknowledge that different religions have adopted their own holy writings to suit their own beliefs.

There was a lady friend who once said to me, "You have made many mistakes, but boy! you have learnt from them." She also told me that I was to stop thinking that I was not as valuable as everyone else; I was at least as valuable as they were. I never forgot that lady, and I have wondered over the years whether she realised just how much that admonition helped me.

My friend Amanda has a good saying: "We are all on the same bus, but sometimes we get off early and go off track."

It's clear that we humans can really stuff up our lives at times. Sometimes we don't return to the bus before our time runs out. But I believe that when we die and look back at our life just finished, along with our guides or councillors, we see where we did well, or maybe where we did not follow our plan.

It's much like looking at our exam marks after a test. This review usually results in another life being planned so that growth can continue. Amanda suggests that we will all eventually get back on the bus or the path in subsequent incarnations.

Most of us don't remember what we have been reincarnated to do, so we can only do our best. If we don't achieve our goals this time, there will always be another opportunity to have a better try in the next life.

Maybe the main reason some people don't like the idea of reincarnation is that this way of thinking makes us realise that we are responsible for our own actions—and, heaven knows, today we all want to blame others for our mistakes!

Having made as many mistakes and wrong decisions as anyone else when I was young and knew so little, I've decided to do the best I can to help others along the way. I would really like to have a rest before embarking on another life. Maybe I set the bar too high this time round, because I have had some tough lessons to get through.

We all know of someone who has gone through many terrible experiences in life, and it seems that there is no way to control them. Even if we could—and many of us certainly would—it seems that we have to go through the experience for a reason.

Helping Others?

I believe that if there are people like me (and there *must* be hundreds and thousands of us) who are using this gift of insight to benefit others, it's not wasted. To have an understanding means not having to repeat the same mistakes. If we ignore what we are supposed to work through, the lesson will keep being presented to us until we do learn, sometimes in different ways. It will be put before us again and again. Sometimes you do get sick of bashing your head against a brick wall. It hurts so maybe we should be thinking about what the lesson is trying to tell us,

Here is an example of using this ability of being psychic to help.

Some years ago when I first moved to beautiful sunny Queensland from New South Wales I knew no one at all, so I joined a gym to meet some new friends. After a few weeks, I got friendly with another lady, and it became a habit for us to have a cup of tea together after our gym session. One day she invited me to her home. She told me that her marriage had recently broken up, and she was not taking it very well.

I had been through this experience myself, and so we talked for quite a while. I went home thinking she badly needed some type of help.

The next day, while doing nothing but staring into space, I suddenly got a picture of her daughter. I had not met this young girl, but in the vision I saw her with a desperate, pleading look on her face. The words that came with this picture were, "You must hold on for me." This worried me a lot, so I tried to call my new friend all afternoon, without success. First thing next morning, I drove around to see her.

When she let me in, I told her straight away about the image I'd witnessed. It was then that she told me she was planning to kill herself but had procrastinated while she tried to think of someone who would care for her daughter. I again shared her daughter's words. I explained that the girl felt that she had already lost her father to another lady, and picking up on her mother's thoughts, she could not bear to lose her mother as well. Her mother had to hold on to life for her. Consequently, my friend did not go through with her planned suicide.

If I had not followed up with what I'd seen, could you imagine my guilt at not saying anything if my friend had killed herself? I am sure we can do a lot of good with these gifts of insight. It was a profound lesson to me to not hesitate in using the gift I have and not to doubt it.

Early Days

When I was younger, I didn't think much about these matters. Even as a young girl, when I got some prompts I usually ignored them and even if I listened, I would always put it down to coincidence. Really, what do you know when you are young. I had no one to tell me anything different. Living in a small country town there was no one who would come forward and admit they had an interest in the psychic. So even if I got something and it proved correct, to me it was just an accident or coincidence. I never thought about it anymore.

I first started to listen to the prompts in my head in my twenties. With my first son I started getting prompts from spirit .I was trying to potty train him and many times I got a prompt to put him on the pot. If I listened and did that, then all would be well, but if I got too busy doing other things and forgot, then I would end up with a wet nappy. This always worked if I listened. At that time I knew that something was going on but still didn't realise how important it was. I remember being told to start writing things down but did not listen even then. Eventually when I was getting a lot of things, I started to keep a journal and have written down many of my dreams, visions, and intuitions.

It was very hard when I was younger and had no one to help me understand these things because sometimes the dreams would make no sense at all, yet at the same time I felt they were important. I have shown very few people my dream books, only people that I feel that I can trust. Even my family have not seen them as sometimes they might refer to them so I kept it secret.

I still use a journal today, so I am able to measure how it has served me well. Many times my dreams, especially, were of great benefit to me, as much as they were in helping others.

Though some of my early notes have been lost, I still have years' worth that I can look back on to see how I've been guided. I've really appreciated the help that revisiting them has given me.

I understand that another thing many people experience, as I have experienced many times, is that we suddenly stop what we're doing and think to ourselves, "I've done this before" or "I've seen this exact event before" and so on. The feeling can be very strong.

I can remember a time when I was about eight years of age and our family didn't have a car in those days and many families were in the same boat. We were travelling with someone else in their car when we were about to round a bend. For some reason I knew what it was going to look like before we turned the corner. I was not surprised when it was as I had envisioned it. Even then I thought it was strange. I knew it meant something was odd but again I had no one to explain anything what this might have been, but it always stuck with me.

It may well be that we *have* done it before, but another reason could be that we are actually remembering some part of the plan we made before coming here. If that is the case, we know we just might be on track to achieve the things that we have been reincarnated for. It's a thought.

My Dad

y father was a troubled man all his life following his active duty in World War II. He returned home suffering from his war experiences, and it was to be a permanent legacy. As part of my inherited nature, I reached out to him over many years looking for the dimension that could only be filled by a father figure. I used to believe that this was why, when I started seeking male companions, they would always be a lot older than I was. As I subsequently accepted more of the philosophy of karma, I expanded on that conclusion.

I remember the day my dad died. I had gone down to Newcastle in New South Wales to be with Mum. That evening, I was in the process of rubbing my mother's feet to help with her circulation, just like he used to, when, quite clearly, someone started to pat my head. I said nothing at the time to my mother. After she went to bed, I went back to the lounge room and sat in my dad's favourite chair. It was about 8:30 p.m.

I was just sitting quietly watching television to take my attention away from my grief, when I suddenly felt someone dragging fingers through my hair. At first, I wondered whether there was a draft playing tricks with my hair and my mind. However, there were no windows or doors open, so I guessed it was my dad reaching out to comfort me.

The next day, I told Mum about something or someone patting my head while I was doing her feet, and she said, "That would be right, he's just making sure you were doing it correctly." She was not surprised at all!

Obedience

But let's get back to the present. After looking around my flat, I sat down on my small lounge and picked up the newsletter from the holiday club that I belonged to.

I liked to dream about these holidays, even though I'd looked at them many times before. I had thought that one day I might be able to afford to go, so I was reading about a particular trip to the UK. Suddenly a loud voice in my head said, "Go book that trip!"

I stopped dead still and looked around, but no one was present.

Then I was told again! The voice was emphatic.

This second time I listened. I had heard this voice once or twice before, and on one occasion it actually saved me from a serious accident. That occasion happened when I was driving home. Normally I trust the indicator lights on other vehicles to clearly show a driver's intention. A car came towards me indicating that it was going right. I too was turning right, in the opposite direction. Relying on its flashing indicators to tell me where the car was going, I went to turn myself—but this voice suddenly shouted *Stop!* I obeyed, slamming on the brakes. The oncoming car did not turn as indicated but kept travelling straight ahead. This vehicle would have hit my vehicle, T-boning me in the middle, halfway into my intended turn.

As this voice had proved to be correct before, I knew I could trust it this time regarding the advertised trip. Even so, I had no money and was living on my own, so I wondered how on earth I was going to achieve this.

I kept reading about the trip and finally convinced myself to make some enquiries about it. I went to the local bus depot the next day to book a seat to Brisbane and was allocated a seat—no trouble. While on the bus, I was thinking and feeling like a total fraud. I remember saying to God, "Well, if you want me to do this, you'll have to make it happen."

In Brisbane, after a long walk, I found my way to the correct office and went inside to the reception area. I explained that I was enquiring about a particular trip, and I was introduced to a travel consultant who would look after me.

When I asked about the trip, the travel consultant gave me a worried look, saying, 'How many seats do you want? I've only got one left."

I started to laugh inside. "One is all I need," I assured her. I knew, absolutely, that the adventure would work out.

Then she added that the tour company in the UK had asked to have any leftover seats returned to them, but in respect to the seat I was allocated, she had said no, feeling certain that someone would want it.

That was the start of that particular synchronicity. I told her I had no money at that time, but my house was up for sale and the funds would soon be available. She told me not to worry, as I only needed a deposit of two hundred dollars. I said okay, even though I knew that I didn't even have that amount. I felt an inner excitement and trepidation as I wondered how I was going to get that sort of money.

I was then nudged to ask whether there was, perhaps, any lady who wanted a travel companion for the trip. Surprisingly, again, she told me there was. By this time, I was feeling really good, thinking that this was meant to be. I got a little bolder and asked about the next leg of the trip through Europe. The consultant again replied, "Yes, the lady wants a travel companion for that trip too."

"Book it," I said and walked away as if on a cloud.

On the way home on the bus, I began to panic. I couldn't see how it could possibly work out. I guess that is what faith is, and boy was I relying on that!

When I got back home, I took my time looking at the details of the trip once more, feeling excited inside. For a long time, in fact for many years, I had believed I'd once lived in a castle, but I did not have any real idea of why I had that belief. I just did.

I felt the same about all things Scottish. I was always picking up kilts from op shops. At one stage, I had at least three kilts, and I still have two of them. I loved the bagpipes and accordions, although I'd never really thought about why, I'd just accepted it. When I first heard the words of "Highland Cathedral" sung, I felt my heart nearly burst with pride. The sound of bagpipes brought tears to my eyes.

My Turn to Be Read

The spiritual church was having a reading day coming up, and my daughter went with me. Many people don't realise that the money raised from these reading days goes to various charities. I wandered around, looking for someone I did not know to give me a reading. Having decided on two different clairvoyant men, I settled down with one for the first session.

This man picked up on my daughter's issues straight away. He advised her to listen to me, as I had not misguided her in the past, as she had erroneously concluded. She acknowledged this assessment. Then the man turned to me and said I was going on a trip, and that I would have a spiritual experience. *Good*, I thought, *maybe I will see a ghost or spirit person!* After about half an hour, I finished talking to him and went to help out in the church kitchen, making cups of tea and coffee for morning tea.

During the second reading, after a few minutes of talking with the man about my family, he said, "You are going on a trip to the UK." I started to answer him, but he cut me off and continued, "I know you don't have the money now, but when the time comes, it will be there." Although this was good to hear, I still had doubts of how this could possibly come about.

I spent the next few days worrying about the money. There seemed to be no way that I would find the funds. Although my house was for sale, house sales at that time were slow.

After much thinking, which only gave me a headache, I decided to ring my son. His business was going well. We had always been close, and he seemed to be the only option I had. I felt really bad about asking for money, but when I mentioned it he unhesitatingly agreed to help.

I first asked if he could lend me enough for the UK part of the trip and assured him that I would be fine with just that. But I added that if he had enough for the second part to Europe that would be even better. He agreed! He knew there would be no trouble getting his money back.

So the first part was taken care of, but the next requirement was funds for spending and food. I couldn't ask for more from my son, so after great deliberation, I approached my bank to get a credit card. After a lengthy discussion, the bank agreed and issued a new card to me. I was really grateful, as I always liked to be independent. Having a credit card meant that at least there was a backstop for emergencies, but I worried that I still needed cash for meals and excursions.

Because of my desire for independence, it was hard to approach anyone to help me with money. It took some time worrying about how I could manage it at all. I could not approach my other family members, even though I knew I would pay them back, so the bank seemed to be the only option. I went back and, because of my good credit, received a loan for the amount needed.

One day the post arrived with my new passport, making the adventure finally seem real—and definitely more exciting. I asked all my family and friends to say nothing about the overseas trip to anyone. With only a few weeks to go, I was amazed at how everything had fallen into place after I stepped out in faith and followed my guidance. That's how faith works. By then, I had plenty of proof. If something is meant to be, a way for it to happen will become apparent.

I remember a few years back when seeing a clairvoyant, one of the things she said to me was some people will only go so far out on a limb, but you will go all the way to the edge and so will achieve more than those who don't take risks. Even so stepping out in faith can still be quite scary. It really is a case of you will see it when you really believe it. And here again I'm doing it writing this book. I've been having some frustrating things happen along the way so I feel like I've really been tested time and time again with my computer crashing, losing my word programme and having to get it fixed at the computer shop. But I guess the saying "in for a penny, in for a pound" has some meaning here. I've already been in for more than a few pennies so I might as well go for the pound. Do or die, I'll give it my best shot.

Finally Underway

The time went so fast, and suddenly there were only two weeks to go. Out of the blue, I received a telephone call to say I had a good offer for the house. A prayer was answered! I accepted the offer, and then I was free to phone my son and give him the good news. I thanked God.

Three days before I was to start my overseas trip, I packed up my belongings and went to my friend's place north of Brisbane and closer to the airport. I could go to the airport with her daughter, who worked in customs at the airport with her own sniffer dog. It really was a heady feeling seeing all that faith coming to fruition. Suddenly I was off.

All of the seniors in our tour group gathered at a designated point in the international terminal of Brisbane's airport. My friend showed off her customs dog to us. When that was over, our group proceeded to the check-in counter.

Later, I stood at the window looking at the jumbo jet on which we were to travel. My mind went back to when I had lived in Sydney many years earlier, before I had my children.

On a Saturday afternoon, my favourite thing was to go to the airport and sit at the end of the runway watching the planes while dreaming of travelling in one of them. Now here I was standing in front of that jumbo jet. What does that say about holding on to a dream? I know they can come true when we truly believe.

These days, I have two visions boards in my craft room. These are just two big pieces of cardboard with drawings and pictures cut from old magazines stuck on them. One is devoted to travel, and the second one has images of the garden I will have one day. I can already cross off some of the things I've achieved.

I have drawn a picture of this book that you are now reading and stuck it on there as well.

Vision boards are just a device to help us keep a positive idea of what we want to achieve. They're another way of having something to look at—for "practical faith." I also have another special board listing the spiritual goals I wish to achieve. However, I know that we must not give up and should believe in ourselves and our dreams so that we can achieve them.

At 4:10 p.m., we boarded our plane and departed from Brisbane. We were given a nice meal, and then we settled down for the night. I was always one for staring out of the window, not wanting to miss anything, as I still do today. When darkness settled, I slipped a sleeping pill into my mouth to try to induce some sleep. But the plane was very full, and sleep proved elusive.

Eight hours later, we landed in Kuala Lumpur, Malaysia. It was quite confronting to see so many Malaysian soldiers standing around with big guns strapped to their bodies. Eventually, we found the bus going to our hotel.

Our ride was quite hairy. With white knuckles, we hung on to the seats in front of us as the bus weaved all over the road. There were no indicators, and it was travelling rather fast. Thank goodness there was not too much traffic at that hour of the night.

We arrived at the hotel at about midnight to the sounds of a big band playing across the street, which kept us awake. We hardly seemed to have had any sleep at all when the phone wake-up alarm rang. We had to be back at the airport early to leave by 9:00 a.m.

We were ushered onto another jumbo jet, but this time it was only half full, leaving us some space to stretch out and try to get some rest. It took hours to cross an ocean, a desert, and then arrive over green countryside once more. But there I was with my head constantly at the window. It was all so exciting.

We finally appeared to be crossing the English Channel. I wondered if it was the White Cliffs of Dover that I could see in the distance. We landed at 2:45 p.m. It took a while to clear customs before being taken outside. The first thing I saw was all these old types of black taxi, and I started to laugh. I don't know why, but it seemed to be just like I'd seen on television many years ago, and I didn't expect it to be still like that.

I felt so happy that I just wanted to get down and kiss the ground—such a strange thing to want to do, but that was how I felt. We were herded onto another bus (we were starting to feel like cattle) and given a short tour of London. It was so strange to see all the street names that are used in the Monopoly board game. As a child, I hadn't appreciated that they were all real places.

My travel agent had given me the phone number of the lady, Mary, who would be my travel companion. I had phoned her before I left and we talked like old friends, so I was really looking forward to meeting her face-to-face in London.

When we reached our hotel, it was beautiful, and just a short walk to Oxford Street. We were given our keys, and I found my way up to my room. When I opened the door, Mary was already there, and it didn't take us long to pick up where we'd left off during our phone conversation.

Mary had arrived much earlier, as she had come from Victoria. I was pretty tired after not much sleep, and my eyes were very sore. Even so, we decided to walk downtown and get something to eat. I still couldn't believe I was in London. The first thing for me, though, was to get to a chemist for some eye drops.

As it only took a few minutes to walk downtown, we saw a pub that we thought looked as good a place as any to get something to eat. We went in and walked upstairs to where they served meals. When we ordered our hamburgers, I asked if they had beetroot in them. The young bloke who was serving us said he was from Australia and no, there was no beetroot. It appeared that a love of beetroot was not shared by the British and was unique to Australians, especially on hamburgers. The meal was so big, with lots of chips that we could hardly get through it.

The smoke in the room was terrible, making my eyes sting and fill with tears, so we left there as quickly as possible. After leaving the Marble Arch area we walked around a lot, and as it got dark, we realised we were lost. We had to ask for directions back to Oxford Street. When we got back to our hotel, we went to bed early, as we had been warned that the following morning would be another early start.

The phone woke me up with a start. I answered it, but it seemed that it must have been our wake-up call. I was a typical first-time tourist—I knew nothing.

We left our bags outside our room and met everyone in the foyer, where we were given our first breakfast in a box. I'd never heard of that before. As we waited, I saw a bus pull up. I wondered if it was for us.

A man walked in and looked around. When he saw me, he stared at me for what seemed like ten seconds, but was probably only about six. I wondered who he was, and if he was going to be with our group. He was. He gathered us around him and spoke before leading us to the bus.

I was still on high, ready for whatever was to come. It didn't matter what it was; I was there for the best experience of my life.

We picked up a few more passengers from other hotels and then headed for the outskirts of the city. My head was glued to the window as usual, although I was talking to Mary all the time. Mary had been to the UK before, so she wasn't a novice like me. She commented on the fact that I was so happy, and she added that she was happy for me. We just clicked so well, like old friends.

Our first real stop was Salisbury Cathedral. It was strange seeing things that I'd only ever heard of. I almost had to pinch myself sometimes to accept that I was really there.

As I mentioned earlier, I love old castles, and churches and cathedrals, too. These were the things I wanted to see the most. With their huge size, these edifices were incredibly beautiful, and something that we don't have much of in Australia.

I was raised in the church as a young person, attending most weeks with my grandmother. I liked the sense of peace I found there. When I started working as a teenager, I slowly drifted away from church life.

The next destination for the bus was Stonehenge— something I was really looking forward to seeing. When we arrived, I couldn't believe the number of tourists crowded into the site. We were given a device to listen to in our own language as we walked the one-way track around the stones. It was very hot, and even though we Aussies were used to the heat, there were others on the tour who were not, and they found it hard going.

We were quite glad to get in the air-conditioned bus and make our way to our hotel for the night. It was such a pretty place right on the coast with pretty white houses all close together, just like the photographs you see in magazines.

After a welcome drink and dinner, we went to bed. We were tired, although I think I was too excited to even be aware of any jet lag. I woke quite early with the seagulls screeching around. Looking at the clock I realised that it was only 3:30 a.m., but Mary was awake, too, so we made a cup of tea and then went for a walk to the water's edge. Coming from Australia, I never realised that many of the beaches in the UK were stony with no sand. It was quite a shock.

It was cool and no one was about, so we wandered around until it was time for breakfast. On board the bus again, we set off for St. Ives—such a pretty place. We had to stay at the outskirts of town and get a small bus down to the main shopping area. I could see there wasn't much room for cars in those narrow streets. Something I was noticing already was that there were lots of pots of flowers all around the small villages, making everywhere look so welcoming.

We had lunch at a sheltered bay and did some shopping, and it was there that I tried my first pastie sitting by the bay as I ate it. This was a lovely small sheltered and calm bay. It would seem like time just idles by here. We were not rushed this time so there was time to look around the shops. St. Ives was quite lovely; I could have lingered much longer there, no trouble at all, but we pressed on, as we still had much to see.

The sightseeing was great, and there was so much to learn. I certainly had my eyes opened, seeing so much more than my own country's vistas. The stories of King Arthur were something I always wondered about; how much was true, and how much had been embellished over the years to make it a tourist destination? At least there was a King Arthur's castle, and the coastline had swirls of mist around the cliff tops, making it seem a bit ghostly.

It was quite a feat, sometimes, to understand the different hotels' room system—they were often quite a maze. We had many laughs trying to find our rooms. Another challenge was trying to work out how to operate some of the showers with all those different plumbing fittings.

Again you realise just how little you know about other countries until you go there. The booking in process, the different way you have keys to get into your room. Not a real key but an electronic card, the layout of the hotels and floors of rooms. I found that I was laughing a lot at these things and just so enjoying it all.

On with the Trip

The Glastonbury stop was interesting. I never studied history at school, but we were always given a talk by the tour guide about each destination. There were so many ruins to see, and as I walked about, I realised there was much contrast between the colour of the ruins and the grass around them. One thing I particularly noticed was how green England was; the drought had been so bad at home in Australia that everything was brown and dry. Here it looked like the landscape had been daubed with green paint.

Bath was an interesting town. Like all tourists, we visited the Roman baths, but I hadn't been aware of those rooms underneath the baths that were used for healings of many types. So many of today's healing methods come from the past, so nothing is really new, it seems.

Mary and I wandered around the shops and got lost again. We had to ask some young girls to help us find our way back. They were so lovely, personally escorting us to our bus. We couldn't wait to get back to our hotel to have a cold shower and change for dinner. Many of the ladies, including me, had swollen ankles. That was strange for me; it had never happened before.

It was really hard to get a cold drink in many shops, as many fridges had open shelves and no doors to keep the cold in. The drinks were at room temperature. Also, the number of tourists was a real eye-opener. I had no idea these places would be so busy. Everywhere we went was full, and queues were common. Still, I loved it, even though it was really hot.

Our next stop was Ireland. I was so looking forward to that. We made our way to Pembroke to cross the Irish Sea. The ferry seemed so big and held so many buses and cars. All this was a real education for me, and I loved it. The crossing was nice and smooth, and when we landed in Ireland, the temperature had dropped about ten degrees, making it lovely and cool, and so green. Someone reminded me why it was so green there: because of the rain. But that didn't worry me at all, as the weather was perfect for being a tourist.

I was so enjoying myself that I completely forgot why I had been brought there. I was beginning to think that I must have simply deserved a good break. We arrived at our hotel in Waterford quite late, about eight o'clock, so our dinner was already waiting for us.

Our guide, Stephen, was very good, a bit like a mother hen looking after her brood. When I looked into his eyes, I felt something strange, but I didn't think too much about it at the time. I was too busy enjoying myself.

Mary and I got on so well that many people thought we were sisters, even dressing in the same clothes one morning by accident. Of course, by this time, people on the bus had made friends and were quite relaxed. It was a nice feeling getting to know all these different people from different countries around the world. By now, it was a lovely group.

I liked crystals, so Waterford was right up my alley with all the beautiful crystal carvings to be viewed. I used crystals a lot with my jewellery-making hobby.

Killarney was the prettiest place, with lots of flowers around the town. The locals seemed to go to a lot of trouble to please the tourists. It was busy and exciting seeing all that.

Blarney Castle was a real test of my fitness, climbing all the winding narrow stairs up to the top. And there was no way I was going to bend down backwards to kiss the Blarney stone! Just looking into the blackness of the dungeons underneath the castle was enough to send me walking backwards. They were pitch black inside.

We had a couple of shows in the evenings, which were a lot of fun. We all ended up singing in the bus on the way back to our hotel.

One night we heard a brawl outside our room, and a girl seemed to be crying so hysterically that I feared someone was going to be murdered. I was so tired that I couldn't get out of bed, but Mary watched and observed for a while. Eventually the police came and sorted it out, and we were able to settle back to sleep.

The next day was another day for visiting a castle, something I never got sick of. I was able to wander freely all around the ruins for a while, but I made sure that I took part in anything that was happening and offered on the tour.

Next, we were off to Limerick. I loved all those castles. At the time, it seemed to be the best experience of my life.

Stephen

A strange feeling came over me when I was physically close to Stephen. There was a definite feeling of somehow being safe and protected. Sometimes when I would look across to Stephen, I would see him looking at me. Maybe I was just imagining it but it seemed that way. I just shrugged it off. Men were of no interest to me. My sister had said to me once that I was a man-hater, and although I didn't think I was that extreme, I certainly had no trust in, or time for, any man. I've always liked men in the past but I just didn't trust them anymore.

Time seemed to go so quickly that we barely scratched the surface of what was available to be seen and experienced. With so much distance on the bus between stops, we didn't really get enough time to explore. Sometimes when we had stopovers of two nights in one place, we could do additional sight-seeing and get our laundry done as well. (At least the hot summer made getting that laundry dry much easier).

We headed for Galway, which I found to be lively. Dublin was our next big stop. One town after another but I didn't mind. These were all placed that I'd only heard of. Our hotel was right in the middle of the main street.

I loved Dublin. There was something exciting about the place—a real vibration—and we couldn't wait to explore it. There was lots of good shopping and places to see.

Mary was tired, but I kept going while she rested. The first night we went to a pared-back version of *Riverdance*. There was a comedian, who was excellent. I hadn't laughed so much in years; how good it was to laugh again! I felt like my old self. In fact, all the performances were wonderful. It was a great night. The previous years seemed to just fade away.

Our driver—Little Tommy, as I called him—was very muscular, and no wonder! He had to get all the luggage on and off the bus every day. He was very friendly and would talk with us whenever he was free. On our way back on the ferry, I told Little Tommy that I loved Ireland and maybe I could just jump off and swim back and marry an Irishman—just joking, of course. But he said, "No, you won't," so that was that.

The city of Chester was something special with all its beautiful buildings. There was a young violin player in the street with a big crowd around him. He was excellent, giving us a wonderful preview of what to expect in the city.

I don't remember much about Manchester. With so many places each day to visit and see, it was no wonder I can't recall them all.

I understand what people say about the Lake District in England being so relaxing and calm. We visited beautiful Grasmere and Bowness. I think I could grow old gracefully there. The lovely wooden canoes were beautiful, gliding along, making not a ripple on the mirrored surface of the water.

Edinburgh was the next big stop for us, with a viewing of the military tattoo. I had only ever dreamt of going to the tattoo. This would be the highlight of the tour for me, because I loved the bagpipes so much. At home, if I heard the pipes, I would follow the sound until I found the person playing, and then I would just stay in the shadows and listen. There was always something calming about the sound for me.

Edinburgh felt really comfortable, with perfect weather for the tattoo. I couldn't have asked for anything better, and our group from Australia was welcomed in the announcements. The displays were spectacular, but the show ended all too quickly. As the huge crowd made its way out of the arena, I wondered how the tour could get any better. Afterwards, many of us met up at a pub. Stephen bought me a drink, and I wished the night wouldn't end, even though it was already after midnight.

Next day, my fitness paid off as I walked around Edinburgh Castle, up and down. Many steps later, I felt I'd had enough, so I went to the local markets on my own.

That night, we all went to another show where the haggis was explained to us—and then we were told they were serving it up. *No thanks!* The music started for the dancing, and suddenly my hand was grabbed from behind and Stephen pulled me onto the dance floor. Again, I had this strange feeling of safety. A song darted into my head: "Can I Have This Dance for the Rest of My Life" by Ann Murray. I felt like I wanted to say the words to Stephen, but I couldn't, as I thought I wouldn't know how to explain how or why it was on my mind.

After the song finished, he spun me around, kissed me on the back of the neck, and said, "I have to dance with the others."

Before I knew it, I answered, "No you don't," but he just smiled and said that he had to. Why did I say that? Sometimes words come out of my mouth so quickly that I don't realise I've said them.

But there was something about Stephen's eyes. If he looked at me, I felt strangely drawn to those eyes. There was almost a knowing, a connection, although it eluded me exactly what those feelings meant.

The night ended on a high, as had many nights. It was hard for me to get to sleep with all the activities that had been arranged for us. We were constantly tired, and by that time many of us couldn't even remember where we'd been the day before. Even so, I would not have changed it for anything. Home in Australia seemed so far away. I just couldn't believe how good this all was. My energy was coming back to me and I felt that I could do anything. Even my back seemed to be giving me a break. Maybe all that walking paid off after all.

A Dream and Confusion

I awoke from a dream early one morning. The dream seemed to be set in the time of the Vikings, and Stephen seemed to be involved. He was protecting me. Is that why I felt safe around him? Strange—there seemed to be some connection, or a sense of protection maybe.

Next morning, I made sure that I would be the last one off the bus so I could talk to him. I told him of the dream, and he just gave me a funny smile but didn't say much. I couldn't blame him for his lack of response, because I had no idea whether he understood such things. Still, I wrote the dream down as usual. My dreams are typically very clear, and usually some significance is revealed, eventually.

Let me interrupt here and mention that outwardly, Stephen had none of the physical qualities I typically found attractive in a man, and anyway, I had no real trust or faith in men at that stage of my life. So, dear reader, please don't even start to think that I was seeking some holiday romance. That was the last thing I needed. Therefore, I was left puzzled about that feeling of being connected with Stephen.

Each morning, we put our suitcases out early and then had breakfast, so that we would be ready for the day ahead. All prepared, we would then go on to our next destination.

We crossed the bridge to the Isle of Skye; however, I decided not to take the extra bus trip around the area because I was so tired. I curled up on a couch in the lounge and let the warm fire send me to sleep. I really didn't want to wake up—I was so comfortable.

Our next stop on the tour, we were advised, was to be another castle, which suited me fine. We all made our way off the bus and across the grounds to the foyer. This one seemed to be more modern. There were groups from so many different countries. I looked up as the local castle guide was talking and welcoming us. My attention was drawn to a huge array of swords hanging on the wall. The local guide's voice faded into the distance as I kept staring at those swords, almost hypnotised, although I couldn't work out why. I don't really like weapons very much, but those huge swords kept drawing my eyes to them. My mesmerised gaze was interrupted when I suddenly heard the guide asking us to follow him.

We trouped up the stairs and I, taking it all in as usual, looked at everything. As I fell a bit behind the group, I came across a life-size soldier in full armour on a horse. I kept looking at it, transfixed, again wondering why I was so drawn to such an image. I just stood there, not knowing why it was holding me so strongly. Why did that particular display have such a hold? It was just a military man on a horse. I didn't want to leave, but eventually, of course, I had to.

The tour continued, and the overall grandeur of the places amazed me. There was such a wealth of beauty and history to be taken in during those limited hours in those too few days.

I came out of the castle and walked back towards the bus. Little Tommy was there sitting on the grass, so we talked for a while until the others came back. As I sat there, my mind unexpectedly flipped back about twenty-five years to when I lived in New South Wales. I lived in a small country town, and I had gone to see a visiting clairvoyant. Even though she picked up about my daughter first, she soon focused on me. Somehow the conversation got onto the UK, and I told her that I had always believed I'd lived in a castle. She told me that if I went on an organised tour, I would find the right castle, and she went on to describe the setting, the green lawns, and how to go over a little bridge to the castle.

And there it was, right in front of me, just as the clairvoyant had prophesied. She had predicted that I would see it "on an organised tour." The tour I was on was exactly what she had described. That certainly was a long-term prediction! How amazing is that? Also, it made sense of the strange experiences inside the castle, of being so drawn to certain things.

Still, apart from that exciting realisation, I was enjoying it all. Sometimes Mary would remark that she was glad I was enjoying all this so much.

I haven't described all the stops, but there was something special about each of them. I loved it all. It's such an eye-opening experience seeing so much different scenery outside one's own country. So much history—something I'd not appreciated before.

Culloden Karma?

We set off for the historical region called Culloden. I'd never heard of it before, and as Stephen started talking about it over the bus sound system, I turned off. Some trigger in my mind had decided that I did not want to listen to the stories of Culloden. Oddly, at that moment, Stephen was insignificant to me as well. I did not like anything to do with war, and since I didn't study history at school, it was of even less interest to me. I just kept looking out the window at the passing scenery. I don't know how long Stephen was talking for, but he had obviously stopped when we pulled up and got off the bus again to go inside a tourist building.

We were advised of the various individual sightseeing options that we could choose from. Mary went off to the movie presentation, but I was not interested in a war movie, so I just stood there thinking about what I could do to fill the time.

Suddenly, without warning, my head started swimming all around, making me feel quite giddy and off balance. *What is going on?* I asked myself. I seemed to be still on my feet, but my head was definitely going around in circles.

45

Stephen came up to me and asked, "Are you okay?"

I replied that there was something wrong, and I would have to get outside to get some fresh air. Without further concern, he left me to head outside and sit on a large rock.

The spinning continued, but in addition silent tears started streaming down my cheeks. *What's going on?* I kept asking myself. The tears turned into sobs, big uncontrollable sobs, accompanied by flooding tears blurring my vision. It was crazy! *What's happening?* I asked again and again.

Strong, most unpleasant thoughts concerning suicide flooded over me, accompanied by an all-consuming pain that hurt me physically. I couldn't understand what was happening. I got up and struggled to the car park where I thought the bus would be waiting, but it wasn't there. On I stumbled, walking around in circles, sobbing my head off. I couldn't stop the tears and sobs no matter how hard I tried. I felt terrible. *Why? Why? Why?* I demanded from the unseen world of the mind.

Stephen walked over to me and asked if I was all right. I felt like such a fool, because I could barely get any words out. I asked him, "What on earth *is* this terrible place?"

He put his arms around me to comfort me, so I blurted out, "I can't help it; I just pick up on things." He said he understood and that I was probably picking up on all the negative emotions from the history of the place. He sounded a little clinical and said that he had to go, but I couldn't stop crying. I kept walking around until the bus came back.

At that moment, I suddenly and unexpectedly stopped crying and lifted my head to look up. Although it was clear daylight, the sky seemed dark, as with a movie screen darkened to enable the clearest projection from a film projector. On that half-darkened screen, to my shock, I saw, like a movie projection, a vision of a military battle. The images were mostly of red-uniformed soldiers. I didn't know what it meant, of course, but as I struggled to understand the profound experience, I concluded that I would no doubt eventually find the answer.

The vision was followed by a powerful feeling that came over me. It was the most powerful feeling I've ever felt in my life. It was like watching multiple doors all opening at once. I knew absolutely, beyond any doubt, that the vision was about Stephen and me. It was something that the normal conscious mind cannot explain. We were together somehow at that particularly dreadful turbulent time in the past. Furthermore, I knew that I would take that awareness with me, in this lifetime, to my grave.

The sense of love accompanying the vision and the revelation was like a physical blow. I had suddenly discovered what "soul love" was, and it knocked me for a six. I knew what the various aspects of love meant on this earth, but they could in no way compare to what I felt then. It was so overwhelming. I had never felt anything like it before. The nearest description is that it was as if all the cells in my body, all the fibres of my being, were exploding with love simultaneously. I struggle to find words to rightly explain how all-consuming, how deep this love was. Nothing seems to fit what I was feeling.

It was as if two connected souls, meeting and recognising each other on this earthly plane, experienced in the recognition an awareness and a quickening that could not be understood by the human mind. It surely can only be the sort of love that comes from many lifetimes together, in various male or female roles.

A spiritual heart cannot be dictated to about who or what to love; it knows in itself what is right. So many things suddenly made sense to me, all in the space of a few minutes. Just as one forms deep attachments and love with one's partner or friends over many decades here on earth, so then it must be with soul families who are attracted to each other by recognition and spiritual love as they choose their specific journeys through time in each existence.

It explained my love for Scotland, the bagpipes, the wonderfully strange connection I felt with Stephen. It even explained my hatred of wars of any kind. I always thought I hated war because of my dad being in World War II and what he went through. Now I could see there was a deeper reason.

A further and terrible revelation immediately following that initial understanding revealed that I was not to have Stephen with me in this life. Our connection was not to be continued on this plane. That was devastating. I didn't know what to do. I couldn't stop crying. I don't think I've ever felt such sadness and pain. To be given something wonderful and have it immediately taken away! I felt totally lost.

I knew I would have to give Mary an explanation as to why I was so upset. I couldn't tell her the truth, of course. Instead, I told her that I would explain it all one day. It was beyond my complete understanding at that time anyway. I'd never felt like that before, and I couldn't tell anyone.

The next few days were dreadful. I couldn't eat, sleep, or stop crying whenever I relived the feelings of Culloden. Although I ached to, I didn't share with Stephen any of my understanding about the connection between us. Every time I tried, I broke down. I didn't give him a chance to share his thoughts and discover his understanding. I didn't know where to turn. It all felt out of control for me.

Nothing in my life could have prepared me for that encounter. As a consequence of my ordeal, I looked terrible. I was so glad to leave Culloden, but it will be in my memory forever.

When we arrived in Glasgow, I couldn't eat breakfast, so I wandered across the road to the square and tried to gather myself together. That didn't work, and I didn't know what to do next. What made it worse was that I knew that in just a few days the trip would come to an end.

I just didn't know what to do. I considered the reality that I would never see Stephen again, which is what the spirit world was in some way telling me. In spite of my yearning, I avoided him as much as possible, in case I broke down in tears.

Surely this was not the reason why I had to come to the UK? How could anything be as cruel as this, to travel thousands of miles and encounter that uninvited vision, and in conjunction with that vision to meet Stephen—such a significant companion from that former life—and then realise that I was not to have him included in my present life? Why? Why? Why? It didn't make any sense. Was God playing a sick joke on me? If I had perpetrated some cruelty involving Stephen in that former life, why was that not revealed to me as well? Maybe I would have a better understanding if that was the case and it was revealed to me.

Did the lessons being played out in the trip have something to do with the feelings regarding suicide as an act of abandonment of loved ones? Would whatever cruel lesson I had to learn be less intense by being given the knowledge of anything I might have originally instigated? Needless to say, I didn't want Stephen to think I was a basket case, but I couldn't trust myself to talk to him without tears. I just couldn't.

My heart really felt like it was breaking with the physical pain. How could anyone ever cope with something like that? Devastating does not begin to describe it.

I was shattered by not knowing how to deal with my lack of self-control, which was compounding my dilemma. There were not enough words, or the right words in our language, to describe this experience, even to myself. So many questions, but no answers would come. Of course, lots of people were asking Mary what was the matter with me, but she couldn't tell them anything. I avoided people as much as possible.

The end of the trip was approaching. What could I do? I didn't want it to end, knowing that I would never see Stephen again. It was more than I could bear to think about. I continued losing weight from not eating, but I couldn't help it. I had no appetite at all.

The last night of the trip arrived, and I was getting desperate to talk to Stephen—maybe there would be some understanding, some release. I missed dinner again. My stomach was in such turmoil; my nerves were jumping like crazy.

I went downstairs to see if I could find Stephen, but I only saw Little Tommy at the bar. I decided I could not afford to waste any more time, so I asked Tommy if he knew where Stephen was. Unfortunately, he had no idea. So I decided to talk to him and brought up the subject of being psychic. He listened intently and respectfully. I told him that I had known Stephen in another life and that I was desperate to talk to him about it. Tommy's answer was to "go and bed him," to which I replied that I didn't need to do that. I simply needed to be held by him and not ever leave. To just melt into and stay in his embrace, find acceptance or whatever, was all I wanted.

I gave Tommy a rough outline of the vision and what I understood from it. At least I could stop crying while talking to Tommy. Surprisingly, he told me about his own unusual experience that he had never told anyone. So we understood each other. We sat there till midnight talking, but I never saw Stephen at all, so I eventually gave up and went to my room.

Next morning, we had a short drive back to our original hotel in London. Again I couldn't eat breakfast, I was so emotionally exhausted and on edge. I had never been so affected by anything in my life, and I had no answers as to what I could do to escape the emotional quicksand in which I appeared to be trapped. It was such a hopeless, desperate feeling, almost like going over a cliff and not being able to stop falling.

Arriving back in London, the bus pulled up at our hotel. Everyone gave tip envelopes out to our guide and driver. When it was my turn, I managed to say to Stephen that I wanted to talk to him inside. I waited around the foyer and saw Stephen waiting at the counter, but as I walked up to him the words left me. I was struck dumb. I was just so sad, trying to keep the tears away.

He just took my face in his two hands, pulled my face up to his, and cuddled me up. Ten seconds of the release I sought—ten seconds of pure joy. Then he let me go. I still couldn't say anything, so I started to slowly walk away. He called out, "Have a good time in Europe." It took all my strength just to nod, I was crying so much.

He stood there momentarily, and then he walked out of my life. The full impact of whatever I needed to experience hit me. I just wanted to die. I felt that there was no point in going to Europe. How could I possibly enjoy anything from there on? I was just a shell, bereft and empty. I watched the bus drive away, taking away any hope for understanding with it. How could this be? I was beyond consolation.

I found a friend I knew I could talk to, and somehow I mustered enough life to buy her a drink and sit down with me. As I shared with her of some of the things that had happened, her husband came with a drink for her; when he saw me crying, he just backed away and left us alone. Being a good counsellor, she listened until I calmed down. I thanked her and then, feeling numb, I walked away, totally lost.

For Mary's sake, I tried to enjoy some time with her. I knew she was curious, and I didn't want to spoil her time by burdening her with my problems. I felt so sorry for her. It was my problem, not hers. I was like a person split in two—one half dying, the other half trying to make the best of the time I had left there. Mary and I had two days to fill before our bus to Europe.

Of course, we had to see Harrods, so we caught the bus there. Harrods was an amazing place. I could imagine how easy it would be to get lost in that store. We have nothing like it in Australia. We saw many other tourist places about which I used to only dream, but most of the time I am sure I wasn't good company. I did so appreciate her for sticking with me. I was going around like a robot by then. Nothing mattered. I kept asking myself why this cruel event had happened to me, but still there was no answer.

Europe

On the first day of our trip, we headed off to board a huge ferry. I never realised how big these ferries were, having only seen them in pictures. It is quite amazing how many buses and cars they can hold. I now understand why there are collisions in the English Channel, especially if it is foggy.

That day, we travelled in brilliant sunshine. It was great to take it in and enjoy it all. I tried to behave as normally as I could. If I felt like I was going to break into tears, I would leave and be by myself. (Bursting into tears with little warning had happened already too many times.)

We landed in France, and I really had to pinch myself. Here I was—a dream come true. The first thing we had to get used to was travelling on the right-hand side of the road. We had an Italian driver, and our bus was a quality Mercedes. We soon made our way into the countryside, and before long we pulled up at our hotel in Belgium, which was quite beautiful. As it was late in the afternoon, we dropped off our gear and were bussed back to the main square to find something to eat.

That was a real eye-opener for me. How little a person understands about humanity and other cultures before seeing more of the world! I really felt that I was in Europe. There were artists all around doing paintings of the beautiful buildings in the square. I'd never seen so many little back alleyways with so many people jumping at you trying to entice you into their restaurant.

Eventually, after asking many shop attendants if they served chicken and chips, I succeeded in obtaining the elusive combination. It was my first real meal in a while, and although I felt hungry, I found I couldn't eat much. It seemed my stomach had shrunk.

The town square was lovely, and many people were occupied doing their own thing, like playing music. It was all so colourful. We spied an Australian ice-cream shop and just had to have one. The lady serving commented that only now was the tourism industry starting to pick up after the September 11 World Trade Centre attack.

The weather again was perfect, but when I was on the bus, in between stops, I just started to cry. I would have done anything to be able to return to the UK and find Stephen. Poor Mary, there wasn't much she could do for me.

One of the first things we noticed in Germany was the excellent roads. We stopped at a roadhouse cafe, had something to eat, and, surprisingly, caught up with some members of the original tour group who were on a different tour.

As we shopped, since we spoke nothing but English, we had to point to things that we wanted to purchase. At least we could read the cash registers in euros, so we could manage the currency transactions. The Germans certainly know how to make pastries. I bought the biggest apple slice ever and had to eat it over two meals. That was in Cologne. At least by then, I was trying to eat.

We took a trip down the Rhine River. It was such a beautiful day, so perfect, not a cloud in the sky and water so tranquil. I asked myself, *Why am I sitting here crying my eyes out?* The stress was eating away at my insides, something I could not control. While such beauty was all around, I felt dead inside. So many little villages, castles, and vineyards all along the banks of the river, yet I could only enjoy it superficially. What a shame! It was what I'd come to see and I couldn't enjoy it as I should have. It seemed so ridiculous to not be enjoying it, but I was barely running on one cylinder.

I had always had romantic thoughts about Heidelberg, and it lived up to the image. The castle on the high part above the city was so big, with thick walls. I imagined it would have been permanently cold within those walls.

When we arrived in Munich, I realised that most towns and cities had a central square where everyone gathered, and there were always many tourists converging there. It was standing room only. There were hundreds of people waiting for the clock to chime and its dancers to come out of the tower and do a little dance. There were beautiful clocks and carvings everywhere.

I managed an apple for lunch. While on the bus, I kept breaking down in tears, but I slouched down behind the seat to hide it as much as possible.

I went into a jewellery store and saw a brilliant Swarovski crystal in the shape of a heart. I had to buy it, and I pledged to wear it around my neck to remind me always of Stephen. I still have it today.

Austria was a real postcard destination—magical and clean. So clean, we could even drink the water from the fountains in the square.

At Innsbruck, our hotel was close to town, so we didn't have far to walk to the central square. We could not have asked for a better location. Mary and I had a horse-and-cart ride up in the hills and through the forest, followed by lunch—not too much food for me, though. There were green forests, the ski lifts were working, and colourful hang-gliders were flying, looking just perfect against the clear blue sky. It was all that one could ask for, and so beautiful. But as always, in the bus I would end up crying and trying to hide it as best I could.

On the way to Venice, we travelled through the beautiful Dolomite Mountains. I could barely see the top of the mountains from my window, they were so high and seemed so white and clean. Although the drive took a while, I wasn't bothered by it, as the views were amazing.

Venice, now that's a place of dreams! This visit was something I'd looked forward to for such a long time, and to finally be there felt unreal. We checked into our hotel and then went by motor boat to St. Mark's Square. It was a night I will never forget. Sitting with a glass of champagne while listening to a big band play "The Blue Danube" was one of the best nights of the tour. I was even able to enjoy it without tears, but the trauma had not left me—someone was missing. If only Stephen had been there with me, it would have been true heaven on earth.

Immediately after each performance and with much applause, the next band would strike up, but it would be on the next stage. This went on continuously, one after the other, all around the square for hours. Everyone clapped after each group finished. It was the best live music I had ever heard.

We needed to return to our hotel, but the accumulated stress was taking a big toll on me. I was feeling so sick that I didn't know how I would make it back onto the boat and then back to the hotel. It was a nightmare.

The next day, I stayed in St. Mark's Square while other tour members took a side trip. It was thirty-six degrees Celsius with no shade. I wanted to go into St. Mark's Church, but the queue was so long I decided to try later. After lunch, I returned to find that the water was rising up from underneath the square, so workmen placed boards over the water for us to get into the church. Even though the water was making my feet wet, I still went in. I sat down and prayed. I pleaded with God, asking Him to bring Stephen back into my life somehow. "Any way, please God, make it possible." I cried until I literally ran out of tears.

I felt so drained I didn't have the strength to get up for a while. There were so many people in the church, I don't think anyone noticed me—I felt very alone. *Was it only a week ago this happened to me?* I asked myself. It seemed like an eternity. I'd had no lunch but just wanted to drink and drink because of the heat.

I must say that the accommodation and meals were of a very high standard. For me, it was such a pity about the meals, because I still couldn't eat much.

Our next destination was Rome and the Vatican, a place most people want to see, and I was no exception. The reality was so much more than any television programme or postcard could show. My mum would have loved to have seen the huge tapestries. As we roamed about all these famous paintings and works of art, we were constantly being told to be quiet, and yet there I was, up against a wall hiding my head, crying. Why couldn't God hear my plea in this of all places? Was my karma that extreme?

The moment seemed to necessitate bringing religion alive in me, even though I didn't think I was religious as such—more spiritual. Regardless, there were no answers to my prayers.

I must have looked awful. One of the men in our group asked me to smile many times and tried to be friendly. I told him something to the effect of "I am heartbroken and need to be left alone." He didn't understand a lot of English and persevered. Mary overheard and asked why I had given that response.

Eventually, I had to ask our guide to tell this man to leave me alone. At least our guide could speak his language.

I had been writing in my diary since the start of the UK trip, and many times that writing was done on the bus. My account was sometimes disjointed because we didn't get much time at night to catch up with our diaries. Also, when in the bus, I could hide my crying behind the book by holding it up in front of my face, which I often did instead of writing.

Back at our hotel, which was wonderful, I went for a swim and was impressed to find that towels were provided.

I'm not used to that sort of luxury, so I tried to make the most of it. Water is therapeutic in so many ways.

When we got to the Colosseum, I found it to be much larger than I had ever imagined. It seemed incongruous that we had to catch a modern lift up to the top of this ancient building. I am distressed by anything that reminds me of man's inhumanity to man, and with that in the back of my mind, I couldn't really appreciate the Colosseum, although I still had my photo taken with a gladiator outside. He asked me where I came from and I told him Australia, to which he replied, "You have beautiful blue eyes." His brown eyes reminded me of Stephen's. I had been pretty good up until that moment, but I emotionally crashed again as the reminder of Stephen opened the wounds I had been struggling to heal.

At the Trevi Fountain, which again was much bigger than I had expected, I threw my coin in, wishing and praying that I'd get to see Stephen again. I couldn't believe that the me I knew was being so pathetic and out of control. Why could I not rein in the emotional turmoil of constantly reliving that irreconcilable, contradictory experience? Why could I not stand back for just a moment and be objective? How long must I be subjected to whatever it was I had to learn?

We went to an Italian restaurant one night, and after we had finished, we were walking along when the man I had previously complained about put his arm around my waist once more. Maybe he was trying to cheer me up, or maybe he was trying to get too friendly. I had initially given him the benefit of the doubt, but when he tried to steer me up an alleyway, it was time to call a halt to his behaviour. I don't know why he bothered really, as I was in no mood for such friendly interaction, which should have been painfully obvious.

As I have noted earlier, the heart has a mind of its own, and only it knows what it really wants. I do not try figure it out. It just seems to know what is right, if I can put it that way. My heart was certainly not open at this time. Until I went on the tour, I had prided myself on being able to reason things out logically, but my reactions to the Culloden experience was something over which I struggled to have any emotional control whatsoever.

I was so tired each night, but to achieve calmness I needed sleep. I would just lie in bed holding the crystal heart in my hand. I couldn't explain this to anyone else when it was beyond my comprehension to start with. The only thing I knew was that I felt that I needed to be with Stephen in some way, and the crystal heart seemed to placate that yearning. There was nothing else I felt but yearning. If I didn't have that, I didn't want to even be in this world.

The heartache was so unbearable. There was just too much pain. I was starting to sound like a parrot, always asking *why?* But never getting an answer. Why couldn't I get some answers from Spirit? I felt like all my confident understanding and ability developed through meditation and prayer had left me, and no guidance was coming through to help me gain control.

Back Down to Earth

Florence, like many other Roman cities, was unforgettable: the statue of David, the beautiful churches, and our amazing hotel. On a lighter note, it was the first time I saw a bidet in Europe. I just started laughing whenever I saw those things. I had never used one and could not imagine doing so.

It struck me that, when so far from home, we rarely heard any news from Australia. Was Australia so isolated? There was no point in watching the television in Italy, as we could not understand the language anyway.

Although the weather was oppressively hot, I did love going to the stalls and markets, as they were really lively and colourful. We headed into the majestic mountains of Italy where it was much cooler and had a welcome break from the heat. Many parts of Italy were so pretty; the lakes were beautiful, and being a gardener, I adored the variety of plants, which were ablaze with colour. I decided that I would go back to Italy again one day and try to see more.

I started to think of getting back to London, and that maybe Stephen would be there with another tour group.

Holding on to that faint hope of reconnection gave me some respite from the anguish of a perceived permanent separation.

Sometimes I would be fine for hours, just enjoying all that I had ventured to see—and then, without warning, I would break down into uncontrollable sobs. How could this be? What underlying deep distress was forever waiting for an opportunity to surface?

As we approached Monaco, we were treated to some stunning scenery along the coast. Big is beautiful there, but maybe only for the well-off, or so it seemed.

We did not go into any casinos, but then again, I wouldn't have known how to play the gambling games, nor did I want to waste my money. We went sightseeing to fill in time before going to the next destination, Nice.

At Nice, we were dropped off in the centre of town—a hive of activity, with music playing in the square. The atmosphere was wonderful. After exploring many shops, we found our way to the waterfront and walked along the promenade to our hotel. It was so hot I wanted to walk over to the water, which looked particularly inviting. I took my shoes off and walked across the stones to feel how the water really was. I couldn't believe it was just stones, not sand.

The water was lovely and warm, but as we weren't dressed for swimming, we continued on our walk. It took us about half an hour to reach our hotel. When we arrived, I changed and headed to the rooftop pool. I soon understood why no one was in the water—it was cold! I didn't stay long, but I did get a drink of Coke, which cost me the equivalent of A $10! As we were travelling first class, our hotel breakfasts and dining spreads were very generous, and fortunately already paid for.

One of the places I loved was a small village about half an hour from Nice with small, narrow, cobblestone streets and lots of arts and crafts.

Our next stop was Switzerland: another dream for me, and somewhere I never thought I would see. Like Austria, it was picture-postcard perfect. It took a while to skirt the mountains and wind our way down to Zermatt. From there, we were put on an electric coach and taken into town. To keep the environment clean, only electric vehicles are used—and it works!

Having checked into our hotel, we raced up to our room. What an amazing view we had of the Matterhorn! We found out the hotel had a pool downstairs, so I quickly changed and made my way there. The water was so warm; to lie on my back and look out the huge windows at the mountain was unreal. How could anything compete with that? What a view! It was heaven, and the memory of it will be imprinted on my mind forever. It even took away the inner pain for a while. I would have been happy to remain there, it was so therapeutic.

I finished off with the spa and then dressed for dinner. After our meal, I walked outside to see the Matterhorn again by night. It was just like a Christmas card, with a bright star and the moon just above the peak. It was a little cold, and the next thing I knew that troublesome man was beside me again. I pointed out the beautiful view and he said, as he put his arm around my waist, "The only thing I can see is your beautiful eyes." It was time to retreat inside again. Not a bad line, though, for a Romeo who didn't speak much English!

Back in my room, I had a strange uneasy gut feeling that something was about to happen, but I had no idea what. That's how my intuition works. It can be frustrating not knowing the specific details.

I only had two hours sleep that night. I was excited about not knowing what was ahead, but I was feeling empty because sleep would not come. Next day, we were off to an early start, as we had a big day planned. We boarded cable cars to take us up the Matterhorn.

At the first level, we waited for about twenty minutes. We were then ushered back into the cable car ready to head to the top. As I looked up, I could not believe we would make it, because it seemed so steep. But get to the summit we did, and there we alighted. A perfect blue sky, snow, skiers going past on the ski-chair lifts—it was the prettiest picture. It gave my brain something to absorb rather than the unreal world through which I was struggling.

Mary and I visited the underground ice caves that had been carved out. I had only seen them on travel shows, and now there I was! Dreams do come true. Although it was really cold, I didn't feel it at all. Even so, you wouldn't want to stay too long in that temperature. I placed my drink on the bar, which was made of ice, and had my photo taken. When we came out, I walked away on my own because I had, embarrassingly, started to cry again. Not only that, I had a crippling headache as well. I took two painkillers to try to dull the pain.

One of the men from the group came over and tried to talk to me. I felt sorry for him, as I could barely look at him for the tears that flooded uncontrollably from my eyes. Thankfully, he seemed to sense that whatever was wrong, it was best to leave me alone, which he tactfully did.

After I regained my composure, I told Mary that I wanted to go up to the top of the building "to see the roof of the world," so I took the lift to the highest level. From there, we were to walk the rest of the way up some stairs. I had climbed just four steps when I became completely exhausted; my heart was pounding so much, I had to stop and catch my breath. I couldn't understand it, as I had climbed up and around many castles without any problem.

I made it to the first platform and sat down gasping for air, thinking that maybe I was having a heart attack. I waited for my breathing to settle down, and then I tried to climb up the next five steps. I could only do one at a time. Eventually, when I got to the top, I tried to stand up. I felt stupid, as the all others in the group seemed to be completely untroubled. I, of course, was forgetting the depleted state of my energy after many debilitating days of stress and not being able to eat anything. After looking around, seeing the tips of the mountains as far as the eye could see, I descended the steps slowly, one at a time. I felt a bit better at the bottom, so I waited until all the others were ready to leave and then I, too, stepped into the cable car.

It is surprising how many people can fit into those cars. Feeling strange, I didn't realise that I had leant heavily against one of the ladies from our group. Then I blacked out.

My next awareness was of opening my eyes, and there I was on my back, on the floor, with someone holding my legs up in the air. I had fainted. As I woke and looked around me, I tried to pull myself together. Who was beside me? It was a doctor, and he was asking me if I had heart problems. No, I said, but then I started crying again, which probably didn't help him to assess my condition.

I tried so hard to stop and answer the doctor's questions. He asked me to move my hands, but they seemed to be frozen and wouldn't work. The doctor rubbed them vigorously until they started to get some feeling back into them. I believe that it was just another example of how I seemed to be looked after serendipitously while on this journey.

A coincidence again? What more could I say? I was very grateful Spirit was continuing to support me by having a doctor next to me when I was so physically down—but still I remained without the help I needed from the relentless inner pressure of my Culloden legacy.

When the cable car got to the next level down, I was given a cup of tea. I waited until the colour returned to my pallid face before re-joining the group. We all returned to the cable car and travelled down to ground level. Finally, I felt so much better. I did wonder how many other surprises were ahead; up to that point in time, I had not done too well.

I concluded that the strange premonition of the previous night—that something significantly unpleasant was imminent—must have been warnings of that cable-car experience. I have since been told that what I experienced was altitude sickness.

When we got back to Zermatt, I walked around until I found a lovely little church. It was quite cold in the shade, so I went inside and looked at all the names of people from around the world who had signed the visitor's book. Then I sat down and prayed through my tears, asking that Stephen would be back at London when we returned.

As a consequence of all the stress, by the time we were due to return I had lost fourteen pounds in weight. I can't remember any time in my life when I had lost so much weight in just ten days because of something that was so hard to bear, much less understand.

Our next big stop was Paris, where our hotel was on the edge of the city and very nice. A big shopping centre sat immediately behind it. After a quick check-in and a shower, we were on the bus again to see the sights by night.

We did a night cruise down the Seine. Our view of the Eiffel Tower was another "pinch me, I must be dreaming" moment. I never knew that it blinked with an array of colourful lights at night. At one point it started to rain, and we took cover.

Our hotels were usually wonderful, and most times Mary and I would get separate beds in our shared room, but this time we got one king-size bed. When I walked into the room, I started to laugh, and Mary asked me why. Then she saw the bed! I was so tired, it just didn't matter. However, it was the cause of many laughs the next day on the bus, after I said I was too tired to sit up all night and watch her. Still, I was on edge every time I had to turn over, just in case I woke Mary. We ended up laughing about it. We were such good mates.

Next day, we went up the Eiffel Tower. The queue was very long, so it was quite a wait to get into the lift, but the view of Paris from the top was breath taking. I hadn't realised how flat the city was. After that, there was so much more to do. The gardens of Versailles were something I had been looking forward to, and they didn't disappoint. The gardens covered such a huge area, and if we'd had more time I'd have liked to have seen more. Classical music was playing all around the grounds, which seemed to suit the setting.

With the beautiful white horses and carriages carrying people around, one could be forgiven for thinking it was another century.

We walked through the palace, and the richness and beauty reflecting those times was nothing like we could have experienced in Australia; it was amazing. The Hall of Mirrors was superb, especially on such a lovely day of bright sunshine. I never knew such places existed.

There was so much of Paris that I still wanted to see, so I decided this was another place I would return to one day. The driver continued to press me for a photo, so I relented and let another driver take a photo of me for him.

The Europe leg of our trip was now finished, and so another bout of nerves upset my stomach at the thought of going back to London. I was hoping against hope that Stephen might be around. The trip back on the ferry was good but my mind wasn't on it. I was dreading arriving back at the hotel and not finding Stephen.

Europe Finished

Stephen, of course, was not there when we returned. I looked around everywhere in vain hope. Why couldn't he be there? I felt so sick and tired, I didn't know what to do. I just didn't want to be there anymore. I didn't want to fight it anymore; it was all emptiness. It was all too hard.

Mary went to meet up with some relatives, so I walked downtown on my own. There were so many people around the High Street, but I felt alone, walking around like a robot not really aware of anything around me. Mary had to go back to Australia one day earlier than me, so I had another full day to fill in alone.

I didn't want to go home to Australia. I foolishly tried to think of some way I could stay in London. But time stands still for no one, and so when the day came I got onto the bus to the airport with a sinking stomach. Surely I would wake up and see it was all a dream. Many of the original group had gone their separate ways, while others had gone on to other trips, so I had to navigate my own way around the airport.

I found my way to the right departure gate, but because it was so busy there weren't enough seats, so I sat on the floor crying—again. I don't think anyone noticed. Crazy thoughts came to me, like *I want to just go to sleep and never wake up, I want to give in*. I did not see a point to the whole episode. I wanted to stay where I was. *Why can no one hear me?* I cried.

A sharp voice announced the boarding of my flight. I still fancifully expected something to happen requiring me to stay, but nothing occurred. I had to get on board.

This was supposed to have been such a dream trip for me, and it started out so wonderfully well. I was so happy—how could it have turned into such a nightmare after only ten short days? I had lost fourteen pounds in two weeks. Nonetheless, I felt like I had found my real home, and I would have given anything to stay.

Back to Australia

It really was a long trip home, although to me it wasn't "home" anymore. I had very little sleep on the flight, which eventually arrived in Brisbane.

After clearing customs and getting my suitcase, I caught a bus to the Roma Street bus station for my connecting bus back home. At the depot, waiting for the bus that would take me those final hours home, I was happy to discover one of the men from our church waiting for the same bus as well, so I suggested that we sit together. After we cleared the city, I mentioned to him where I had been and told him I'd had "an experience" there.

He looked across at me and said, "Yes, a past life."

I could only nod. So I said, "I know how I died."

To which he astonishingly responded, "Yes, a sword through the heart."

I just nodded. I already knew from past experience that he was psychic, so his comment didn't actually surprise me.

I couldn't add any more to the conversation because of the tears. I tried to change the subject for at least a while, because

I needed to think. It felt like Australia was not my home anymore. The soul-searching questions kept racing across my mind: Why did this happen? What was the reason for it? To go on a great adventure only to return home heartbroken? I didn't even like men before I left Australia. I was carrying too many scars, yet I instantly knew I could have trusted Stephen with my life. How does a person get over something like that?

Finally, I was back in my flat. I looked around; it all seemed so empty and quiet. What was I going to do now? After all the unpacking, I sat down with my dream book, opening it at the last entry I had made before my trip. Two weeks before I left, I had written about my dream of a man with whom I was walking. I was simply stunned. I just stared at the entry. It was a description of Stephen, exactly as he was in real life.

I had long been dreaming every night and recording the dreams. After that, I wouldn't think much about them until something relating to them manifested itself. So I had just forgotten that particular dream, as usual. I had never even thought about it until I read it again after arriving back home in Australia. With the advantage of hindsight, the only detail not correct was that in real life, Stephen is a bit taller than he was in the dream. But apart from that, he was exactly the same.

In the dream, I was going to introduce him to my parents but went past them, saying to him, "I can't introduce you to my parents because I can't remember your name." Of course I couldn't, because at the time of the dream I had not met him yet.

To this day, I can still see that dream in perfect clarity. To me, it was so clear that I was supposed to meet him—but why meet him only to then not continue to be with him? It just didn't make any sense. It was all too much, and the pain started again. When I picked up my photo of him from the tour, the pain was overwhelming. Surely this must be what a heart attack was like. How much stress could one body take?

When my friend Harry told me before I left that I would meet a man with grey hair on the bus, I had thought to myself, "Yes, a bus full of all different people, there will surely be a man with grey hair." I didn't place much importance on that statement. As I reflected further, I saw that the first thing I needed to do was to get Diane to arrange a reading with her friend Patsy as soon as possible, which she did.

My reading was held at Diane's shop. After I sat down with Patsy, she picked up on what had transpired straight away. I found it so hard to talk for the crying. She said, "Yes, you thought he had died, and so you killed yourself." This made sense to me. That was why I was picking up all the dreadful thoughts concerning suicide at Culloden. She asked me if I had been a Jacobean, but I didn't know what she meant.

At times in my current life, when problems seem insurmountable, I recall with some concern that suicide had crossed my mind—even though, in truth, it was out of character for me. Patsy changed her approach and went on about how I loved the pipes and drums. She confirmed all that I had thought about being with this man in the past, but that was no comfort to me in respect to how I was then feeling.

She also said that there would be a book, but I ignored that.

More Confirmations

Over the next few weeks, many of my psychic friends made comments in a similar vein. Some said I would be with Stephen, which is what I wanted to hear, although I could not see how. Still, it was my hope that they might be right, and any hope was worth clinging to.

Soon after I got back, I attended our usual meditation group again. I told them my story but deliberately didn't mention any names. When Harry offered the word *Culloden*, of course I had to confirm to the group that he was right.

After a few weeks, there was a mind, body, and spirit festival being staged in town, so I went along. I didn't want a reading, but as I walked through the stalls, a lady pulled me aside and said, "I need to pull that sword out of your shoulder." I immediately knew what she was on about, so I let her go through the motions of pulling out the sword. I thanked her after sharing a little about my past life. Then I left, reinforced with the knowledge that the confirmation of the insights by so many others was something I could build on as I struggled to deal with it all.

Many times psychic people, uninvited, stopped me wherever I was, finding themselves compelled to tell me what they saw had happened to me. Some told me I would end up with Stephen, some not. I didn't approach any of these people—they came to me. It might be assumed that these people, by adding their confirmation, would help me. But just when I thought I was getting better, someone would bring up the subject and I would get upset all over again. I wondered when this would ever end.

Of course, word had spread about what had happened to me, so there were many curious people asking about it. I was always crying, and to this day I don't have any control over it. I still don't understand why, even now. I was very self-conscious about always being in tears and was getting sick of it. My body still had not recovered any of my lost weight. I'm not a big person, and losing so much weight made me look painfully thin. Though I tried, I still couldn't eat much.

Many friends suggested that it was a karmic experience. Meeting and being reunited with Stephen and then being completely ostracised from him was similar to losing a loved one through suicide, which leaves those remaining devastatingly bereft. It made sense, yet it was not what I wanted to hear. I so much needed to be with Stephen, to be held by him and not let go.

Meeting Lizzie

A few months later, I saw an advertisement in the local paper about the Royal Scots Dragoon Guards from Scotland coming to Brisbane for a concert. I had to go. A desire to hear the bagpipes enveloped my entire being, I booked a seat right in the front row and found myself on the bus to Brisbane once more.

On the day of the concert, I was escorted to my seat. I looked behind me and saw at least twelve rows, all empty. *Maybe people don't like Scottish things as much as I do*, I thought. Then I saw the usher leading a Marilyn Monroe lookalike to a seat near mine. She came right up next to me. Just to be friendly, I introduced myself. She said her name was Lizzie.

I said, "Someone else who likes the pipes like me?"

"Yes," said Lizzie. "I love all things Scottish."

I mentioned that I'd just been there, and Lizzie asked if I went to Culloden. I just looked at her and didn't know what to say at first, and then I said, "I've been here and there."

But she cut me off, saying, "Yes, but did you go to Culloden?"

It was as though I was struck dumb and couldn't speak.

She asked, "Is your birthday in October?"

Suddenly I knew what Lizzie was about; she was also psychic. So I said, "Yes, my birthday is in October, and, yes, I've been to Culloden."

She responded, "Yes, I know, you found your love, you found your home."

Well, that was enough for me. The tears started again. I just kept looking at her, a bit lost for words. We were interrupted by the pipers who had walked on the stage and were starting up. Suddenly, it was double tears from both of us.

At intermission, we went outside and Lizzie bought me champagne. She proceeded to tell me all about the past few years of my life, describing it perfectly. Lizzie kept telling me how much I had loved this man in Scotland at that time, and that he had come into my life to "open up my closed heart again to men, to enable me to love again." The only trouble with that was I wanted to be with *him*.

We were meant to meet for a reason. I don't believe in accidents. Synchronicity was still at work. What were the chances of meeting up with someone like Lizzie unless it was meant to be? We became friends from that day on. We both loved the concert and had much to share about our trips to Scotland. She asked me to come down to Brisbane to spend a day with her, which I agreed to do.

The following week, I visited Lizzie in her apartment right on the Brisbane River overlooking the Storey Bridge. It was quite high up, so the view was breath taking. We played bagpipe music, danced, laughed, and at times she had me crying. Also, she did a reading for me. She did not tell me what I wanted to hear, although I knew she was right anyway. After having a good day, and I think a few too many glasses of champagne, which really affected me (as I don't usually drink), I thought I should go home.

Before I left, she mentioned she was going overseas again and needed someone to house-sit her cat. I was a free agent and told her I would do it for her. I would love to spend some time in Brisbane sightseeing. So that was settled.

She was to contact me sometime before she left for overseas. One day, she rang and asked me if I would like to do a steamboat river cruise with her and her husband. It was something I'd never done before, so I said I would love to. On the day, I drove down to Brisbane and met up with them. Although I didn't know what to expect, she asked me to just bring a cooked chicken, as she didn't eat much of the food the cruise boat had for lunch.

"No problem," I told Lizzie, but I also packed in some sunscreen, something she was grateful for later, as the sun was very hot.

It was such a lovely day, cruising right out to the mouth of the river where we dropped anchor and had a barbecue lunch. The open sea was calm. The steamboat was staffed by volunteers, and the smell from the barbecue that the men had cooking drifted up from the kitchen to the deck where we were sitting.

What a great way to spend a Sunday. Lizzie was an outgoing person and soon struck up a friendship with some of the crew. There were a few different nationalities on board, one being a Scottish man called Jim who she got to chatting with. We talked for a while until afternoon tea was served. A lovely piece of cheesecake in a cane basket arrived for each of us.

I hadn't realised how much activity there was on the river. There were big tankers and ships passing as they left port on their way out of Australia. Small boats and ferries were all doing their own thing. There was such a feeling of freedom, just to be doing what you like for a while.

Back home again, I thought about writing to Stephen, so I just penned a small note. I didn't really expect an answer, and I didn't get one, but after a while I decided to write again, explaining what had taken place for me there. I even mentioned dreaming of him two weeks before I left. I waited but got no answer. I really wasn't surprised, I just hoped he didn't think I was some weird person. He saw what had happened, and if he didn't want to know, then there was not much I could do about it.

Finally, I decided that I would have to go back to the UK before I could put an end to this situation. In the meantime, Lizzie thought I needed to clear my mind on the history of Culloden. She purchased a book about the events of 1745 that she hoped would help me in some way. However, whenever I thought about picking up the book to read it, I couldn't. The resistance arose out of a feeling of fear, of possibly going through all the pain again. I didn't want to read the story just to feel worse. I dreaded any new information. The book is still in my library; I can't throw it out, but I can't read it either.

I also can't watch anything on the television about war. Delving into the history of Culloden I am sure would only intensify my inability to deal objectively with the subject. For this reason, I understand why sometimes it's not good to know all about our past lives.

Making Plans

Harry rang me one morning and said he was going over to another spiritual church to learn reiki and would I like to go with him? I felt that this was something I could use, so I went. It took us more than an hour to get there.

When we arrived, there were quite a few others there as well. After a couple of hours, we broke for lunch. I took the minister aside to tell him that I'd had a past-life experience. He simply said, "Culloden."

Here we go again, I thought.

He continued, saying, "Yes, you were the son and he the father."

To which I replied, "Yes, but I love him as a woman would love a man."

"Love is love," he said.

That stopped me! It made sense of many things. Whether between a husband and wife, father and son, brother and sister, or even just best friends, love is still love. I could now understand why, when I went for the first reading on my return to Australia, I was told that because I thought my father had died, I had killed myself—but in fact, he did not die. It made so much more sense that if he, my father, had lost me, his son, then maybe this time around I had to know how I (the son) would feel losing Stephen (the father) to appreciate the grief I had caused by my suicide in that lifetime.

I certainly would not have been on the battlefield if I had been a woman, so this made a huge difference as to how I consequently looked at the matter. I was still human and still felt the emotion, but I understood more clearly now and maybe I could live with it after that understanding. It is said that time heals all wounds. I sincerely hoped so, because at times I remained inconsolable and did not understood how I could ever see an end to it.

Harry and I finished the day off and headed home. Nearing home, I suddenly felt someone patting and stroking the back of my neck. It was unnerving, so I mentioned it to Harry, and he just casually said, "It happens." So I knew someone was still looking after me, even if I didn't know exactly who it was.

Reiki

It was good to have the certificate to perform reiki. I'd always wanted to help others in some way, and I thought reiki might be it.

One day, Harry announced to Diane that he would be leaving and heading south. This left Diane having to pay the full rent for both flats, which was quite a burden. She didn't know anyone wanting to share with her.

About six weeks later, I answered a knock at my front door. My landlady told me that her son owned my flat and he needed to have it back, so I was given plenty of time to find somewhere else to live. As usual, fate had stepped in, and of course it was ideal for me to move in with Diane. I put all my things in storage and moved in. She was a fellow Libra, so we got on beautifully.

From there we had the meditation in my end of the house, as I had a lovely big log fire for the cold winter nights. It's really funny how both of us Libra personalities were so similar. We both discovered that we had worked in a movie theatre. We both always took the third slice of bread from the top of a loaf. We both liked to dress well. We both liked jewellery, and later we took that up as a hobby. If she was late home from work, I knew that I could cook a meal and it would be something she could eat. Of course, justice and fairness were paramount in our life, and our catch cry was "That's not fair."

Most days I would walk to the shopping centre not far away, and I always passed a home with a beautiful garden. I would stop and talk with the owner, Dave, and we became regular communicators, conversing about all things garden. His garden was much bigger than mine, so he had a much bigger display; he was retired, so he had the time.

One day he stopped me and said, "I have cancer." I looked at him and knew straight away he wouldn't make it, but as he was a big burly man, I just told him that all he could do was fight it. I believe we must never take away hope from anyone.

Suddenly my arm started to shake, and I wondered why. After a few more minutes of chatting, I started to walk homeward, but still my arm was shaking. When I got home, I thought maybe Spirit was telling me to use reiki on Dave. This became a very strong feeling, so I walked back to his place and asked him if he knew what reiki was. He'd never heard of it. After explaining all about it, I told him to mention it to his doctor.

A few days later, Dave pulled me up. He had followed this up with his doctor and was told that the doctor himself did it but didn't have the time. If I could do it for him, the doctor advised, then go for it.

My first session with Dave was a good start. After I showed him how it went, while his wife looked on, I could certainly feel the heat in my hands. This became an everyday event, and he said he was starting to feel a benefit. That's all I wanted. If it helped his pain, then it was worth it. His son, however, thought it was a lot of rot.

I told Dave I was on my own and just lived one block up the road. If he ever needed me, day or night, he could ring me, and I meant it.

A few days later, Dave said his son was going to ring me. I did wonder why. Perhaps his son was going to have a go at me? But no, it seemed his dad was in so much pain he was willing to forget his attitude. In the end, though, no one rang. When I asked why, Dave said he didn't want to wake me in the middle of the night. I gently scolded him, saying I would have come, and he shouldn't hesitate again when he needed me.

It had been suggested to him that he should have a second round of chemotherapy, but he had declined because the first ten sessions had knocked him around so much. He was at peace with that.

After some weeks, I had to tell him I was returning to Scotland. His wife wanted to know if she could do the reiki treatment in my absence. I showed her as best I could and wished him well. I wondered if he would still be there when I got back, as I would be away for six weeks.

Going Back to Scotland

I made my booking, and this time I chose to stay at different bed and breakfast places (B & Bs) in Scotland. I left two full days in London to arrange them.

Amanda and Robert were a couple I had met through the church. They had been attending our meditation group, which was still going strong at that time. One night when Amanda and Robert were there, I was going around the group as usual and received a lot of information regarding Robert. I asked him about what I had "read." Amanda remarked, "If you only knew how many things are wrong with him," but I did know, as I could see it.

On another occasion, I was concentrating on Robert when I immediately saw an image of an old-fashioned monk wearing a worn brown robe with a rope belt. He was walking around what seemed to be a monastery. So I described it.

Amanda interjected that the monk was their spirit guide, and that they hadn't heard of or from him in quite a while. In my own meditation, I saw Stephen and me sitting on the ground with our legs crossed like children. There was the sound of a muffled drum, and when I looked up I saw the outline of two gold hearts, one crossing through the other as it floated down to us and the words "Two hearts beating as one" to the same beat of the drum in sync with the vision. It was beautiful. The next day I went downtown and had that scene tattooed at the bottom of my back as a permanent reminder.

In another meditation, I saw what I believe were the grounds of a castle that I had visited. Stephen and I were walking the grounds together—although he looked physically different, the eyes were his eyes. He had soft brown curly hair and was dressed in the style of the period. I, a female, had a lovely full-length gown on and was walking with my arm looped through his. It was a very peaceful, happy scene.

This scene reminded me of a time in 1998 when I had my first palm reading. After some time, the palmist mentioned a previous life and described me and my husband. I was wearing a full-length gown and was married to a rich merchant. This reading was written down at the time, and I still have it today.

When I was a young girl at primary school, I used to go to the library and draw pictures of the ladies in their long gowns. I never changed the style. If I wasn't playing sport, that's what I would be doing.

Now, the palmist's reading made sense.

The time for my proposed trip was fast approaching. A week before I was due to leave, I became really upset, crying again, telling Diane that I knew, even though I really prayed for a meeting to come about, I was not going to see Stephen again. I couldn't help it, I just knew—but all had been set in motion, so I might as well try to enjoy the adventure this time around.

Once again, I made the long trip to London, but not with any great excitement this time around. When I landed in London, I found the first place where I was to stay in the city, settled in, and then walked downtown to find something to eat. The flight had been much more enjoyable this time, and I wasn't so tired.

Next morning, the nerves in my stomach were at it again. I wanted to phone Stephen and just talk. I picked up the phone and dialled. He answered. I asked if he was busy and was told that he was. I said I would call later.

I waited until after dinner and tried again. He answered, and when I told him who it was, he didn't give me a chance to talk before blurting out, "I am married, and you are just a client."

I saw red and thought, *how arrogant of him.* I had not even been given a chance to get a word in. I replied, "Stephen, don't worry about it" and hung up. After the call, I sent a text saying "I wanted nothing from you other than to talk. You won't hear from me again." I added, "I'll see you at the end of this life. Off to Scotland." I felt cured of any delusions in the space of one minute.

Of course, the rebuff hurt, but I wasn't going to waste any more time pursuing what Stephen was satisfied to deny. I walked a long way until I found the Scottish Information Centre.

Stephen's choice was, I suspected, an unconscious one— but if not, surely he would be subjected to similar pressures to the ones I had experienced until the karmic consequences had been fulfilled. The laws of the universe are immutable.

It has been suggested to me many times that Stephen would have had the same nightmare—of a battlefield where he stood over a young soldier whose face would have made him scream with anguish. The young soldier would still be clutching the sword that had been thrust into his chest. Stephen would deny any reality by imagining that such a recurring dream had been stimulated by his work as a guide at Culloden (or, as he had said, "picking up on the history of the place").

When he met me, he seemed to initially have had a feeling of welcome, but at the same time, it seemed as though something inexplicable would unsettle his peace of mind, and he would depart.

Some Degree of Freedom

At the Scottish Information Centre, I was given a list of B & Bs. I rang one straight away to make a booking.

Doing things on my own was very different from taking an organised tour. With no one to arrange everything for me, I had to carry my own luggage, book the train, find a taxi, and get straight to Edinburgh as soon as possible.

I like train trips, and it was a relaxing trip to Edinburgh, the scenery ever-changing. This time, travelling on my own, I felt different. Last time I had been so happy at the beginning but ended up so sad and desolate. I was determined to stay positive this time.

I caught a taxi to my accommodation and booked in. The lady was lovely and very helpful. It was late in the afternoon when I arrived, and I needed to find some food. There was a pub a few doors away, but when I went in, it was full of men watching football, which made me feel rather uncomfortable. I ventured further until I found a small corner shop, where I bought a few groceries.

I had booked in for two weeks, so I had plenty of time to explore. I felt very much at home. First thing next morning, map in hand, I set off for the city. It was a lovely walk and took about half an hour. When I reached Princess Street, I heard the faint sound of bagpipes, so I kept going until I found a piper busking.

What a beautiful picture. He represented all that I love about Scotland, so I just stood aside for a while letting the sounds soothe my sad soul. Suddenly, a strange and strong feeling came over me, all through my body. Again, a knowing, an attraction—I couldn't define it, but I'd learnt to recognise it, and it was definitely not the usual type of feeling when you just meet a stranger. It's when you meet someone you have known before. I watched as tourists had photos taken with him and thought I would like one, too. Another tourist asked me to take a picture for her with him, and I did, and then she in turn did the same for me.

I dropped a donation into his case and listened for a short time before setting out to explore the city. I headed up to the Royal Mile. I loved all the cobblestones, the ancient buildings, and everything about that area. It felt so comfortable and exciting at the same time.

Later, when I walked back downtown, the piper had gone, pity. I would have stayed for some more music. I found my way home and went down to the pub again. This time, there was no football crowd in attendance, so I went inside and ordered a meal. When it came, though, I could hardly eat anything.

The lovely girl who served me was concerned that maybe the food was not right, but I assured her it was just me. I asked for some dessert, and she brought it to me, refusing to charge me, even though it wasn't her fault that I couldn't eat.

Next morning I went into town, hoping to see the piper again. He turned up at about 11:00 a.m. I stood to one side to listen, but he noticed me there, and when he had a break he asked me if I had been there yesterday. I replied that I had. He said that he was taking a break shortly and would I like to join him for a cup of coffee? Of course I would.

We walked across the road and sat down in the shopping centre. After ordering our drinks, we introduced ourselves. His name was James, and after a bit of small talk, I mentioned how at home I felt in Edinburgh. He said, "That's because you've probably been here before."

I smiled as I realised that here was another person put in my path who knew what I meant. "Yes," I replied. "I found that out last year when I was here." I gave him an abridged version of what had happened, and he wasn't at all surprised. We found that we could talk a lot about this subject, and I told him about my interest in the spiritual.

His time was up quickly because he had to go back to busking. I gave him my phone number and knew I'd made another friend.

It was good to make a friend so quickly, because he could help me with places to visit and buses to catch. I met up with him quite a few times for a drink. With all this walking, my back was getting sore. I mentioned this to James, and he said he performed healing.

Here we go again, I thought. *Just the right person at the right time.*

He suggested he could come over to my room and do some healing on me. This was one approach I hadn't heard before, but I went ahead anyway. Even after a few minutes, I felt the effect. I seemed to be a bit light-headed, so he stopped. I mentioned that I would like to find someone who did massage, but he didn't know anyone so I left it at that.

The next day, I asked him where I could go for some good bagpipe music and he told me of a *ceilidh* (pronounced *kay-lee*) that was happening just up the street the following night.

I turned up as directed and paid my money, and I made sure to tell the lady at the door that I was visiting from Australia. She took me by the hand, introduced me to some people, and told me they would look after me—and they certainly did. They wanted to know where I was from and made me feel right at home. The welcome was warm, even though my feet were freezing.

The guest artist, a piper, was playing the bagpipes, and for the first time I heard someone singing the words to "Highland Cathedral." I felt a surge of pride almost bursting from my heart. I had a great night and caught the bus home.

Having read *The Da Vinci Code*, I wanted to see the Rosslyn Chapel. I found the bus stop but had to wait almost an hour for the bus. Eventually, though, I did get there. It was almost lunchtime, and after stepping off the bus, the first thing I saw was a pub. I walked over, and by the front door they had a menu on a stand. The first thing I saw advertised was an Australian T-bone steak! That was good enough for me.

The pub itself was beautiful, with highly polished rich red timber. The armchairs were big and comfy, just like the old leather chairs of the past. Heavy curtains hung all around, completing the picture. When my steak arrived, it was huge—much better than we get at home. In fact, I couldn't finish it. I usually love my sweets, but I couldn't fit one in! With the meal finished, I set off for the chapel. It did not disappoint.

It was such a small church, totally different from any other—and I had seen many on my tour the year before. The carvings were amazing. You would never see that type of talent today, and I've certainly not seen it anywhere else. I explored the remains of the small castle behind the chapel and then caught the bus home.

James and I were sitting in the park while on a break, and he mentioned that he had lived in Australia for a short time. It had also come to me that we may have been siblings in a past life, but I didn't suggest this to him at that stage. Sometimes, at night, he would do deliveries for his clients, so I went with him for something to do and to get to see Edinburgh by night. We usually went on foot, but sometimes we caught a bus. We were lucky with the weather being so fine.

Going Back in Time

One day, James asked me if I would like to explore the past. I agreed.

We walked to where he knew of an office he could use up on the Royal Mile and got seated. I noticed a box of tissues on the desk. He started to ask about the experience the year before. As I got to the place where I had to say goodbye to Stephen in London, the tears started.

I said, "I've seen that look on Stephen's face before."

James told me to go back in time. Instantly I went back—to the battle scene. It seemed almost dark with little light, and all I could hear was an eerie silence accompanied by a few low groans. I looked around and saw many men prostrate, mostly dead. I was looking for my father, but I couldn't see him. I was sobbing again. It was such a terrible feeling of being alone. It was too much. I was as emotional as ever.

James said, "Go back further."

Instantly, I saw myself as a young boy, about eleven years of age with ginger hair.

James asked, "Where's Stephen?"

Although I couldn't see him, I knew he was around somewhere, and I felt no sense of fear. I saw how I was dressed—in farming clothes, it appeared—and I was on a farm or somewhere similar. I wanted to leave this scene, so James clicked his fingers and asked where I was now.

I was on the edge of a body of water, more like a bay leading to the sea. I was one of many women, and we were standing around waiting for boats to return. Most boats did, but none came for me.

James asked me to describe what was happening.

I said I was standing alone; I had just sunk to my knees crying. Whoever *he* was had not returned, and I wondered if this scene was attached to the dream of Stephen being with me in the time of the Vikings. That was a dream I had experienced during my first trip to the UK.

James told me to go forward again and asked what I could see.

I told him I couldn't see anything, because in my visualisation I could not move. The fog was so thick I couldn't see anything, and I was too frightened to take even a single step. I was too scared to move.

Now that interested me. In my present life, I had always been anxious about being in thick smoke or heavy fog, especially at night when I went to bingo. I lived on the edge of a range, and many times the fog would be so bad I had to feel my way along the edge of the road to find the side markings. Once we understand where and when a fear is born, we can decide—and it is a choice—that we don't have to be bothered by it anymore. If we have had an unreasonable phobia or fear in this life that we cannot explain, if it can be traced back to a past life and understood, we have the choice to free ourselves from it. We don't have be permanently burdened by the phobia.

This problem has been explored a lot in modern times by using hypnosis to uncover fears that come from a past experience in a past life. Fears that are still having an effect in this life and are holding people back often come out as a physical problem, such as marks on their shin or rashes and unexplained body problems. There are many books that have covered this area of study, so it's certainly worth thinking about, especially if you can find no other answer.

We continued our work together for two more nights, and I felt very tired from all the tears. I didn't want to do it anymore, and I didn't want James to think that all I ever did was cry. It was not a good memory for him, and I was still struggling to get over it myself.

I understood then where my feeling of being alone in this life originated. I said to James that the pictures I saw were so clear that I could see no reason to doubt that conclusion.

I mentioned that I was going to go to Inverness for a week. I'd made arrangements to go by train again. The night before I was to leave, I started to get a big dose of nerves in my stomach, and I thought, *Okay, what's coming next?* Nerves were usually a sign that something significant was about to happen.

Inverness

The next morning, I boarded the train and set off into the countryside. I saw lots of white covering the fields. I thought this might have been snow, as it was getting much colder by then, but an English couple sitting beside me explained that it was just frost.

It was a lovely trip and took about four hours. After I got off the train, I wandered up to the taxi stand. Instead of my nerves getting to me as anticipated, I had a surprisingly good feeling. I felt happy, and I wondered why I had been so on edge the night before.

At the taxi rank, the driver helped me with my case. After a short ride, I was dropped off at my B & B.

Although it was after lunch, I decided to go and explore the town. It only took about ten minutes to get there. There were bands playing in the streets, which to me seemed like a good omen; it gave the place such a boost of happiness. I loved to explore new locales, so the time went quickly as I established the basic places that I would visit the next day.

By about 3:00 p.m., it was already getting cool, so I headed back to my B & B. The next day, I went back into town to find the Tourist Information Centre. One thing on my agenda was to visit the famous Findhorn, a special, widely known spiritual place. There were many other activities available, but as it was late in the season, some of the tours had closed. There were some that I could do, but the first thing I had to find out was how to get to Findhorn.

I had read a book about Findhorn before leaving Australia, and it had really impressed me. I remember commenting to a friend when I first picked up the book that I had to visit there. I don't know why I said that, but I felt strongly about it, so I put it on my agenda. It's amazing what can be achieved if we listen to Spirit as the people at Findhorn have done.

Agriculture is very hard physical work in this harsh climate. It is so cold you would think it impossible to grow anything at all, but at Findhorn they certainly did, and very successfully, with stunning harvests. In the early days, people came from all over the world to see these gardens, and still now they are very well known as the residents carry on with the work.

The next day, I boarded a bus and set off into the countryside. The scenery continued to be beautiful, with pretty flowers adorning the small towns. Just a short distance from Inverness, I saw a sign pointing to Culloden. *That's why my nerves were on edge.* I had honestly been quite ignorant of the fact that I was near the place.

I got off at a lovely place called Forres, and because I had time before the connecting bus would take me to Findhorn, I walked around the cobblestone streets and called into lots of shops. It was such a pretty place, with flower beds in all the streets. From a tourist's point of view, they certainly went to a lot of trouble decorating their town. It was great! Maybe another time I would make a great travel guide, as I loved the job of making people happy about their holidays and pointing out all the positive details about things and places. Just dreaming.

Elgin was another pretty village to wander around in, and I found a religious garden and other ruins to explore. I did wonder if the residents took their environment for granted. I knew I wouldn't if I lived there. It was lovely. Maybe it appealed to me because I'm a gardener at heart.

There's something nice about being on your own and having time to look around everything. When I arrived at Findhorn, there were only a few people around to ask where I had to go, so I walked along the water's edge until I heard sounds coming from a hall. When I walked up to the door, a lady came to help me. I told her where I was from and that I was looking around. Scottish hospitality took over, and she warmly welcomed me inside, gave me a cup of tea, and sat me with some ladies to talk.

When the time came to leave, I really wished I didn't have to, but I wanted to find the spiritual centre. Because it was late in the season, there were not many visitors, so I was free to look around by myself. I felt a little disappointed, because it was really quiet, with very few people around to pass the time with or talk to. Instead, I filled in time at the gift shop. A lady from Australia was a member of staff there. One thing about the Findhorn community, for sure, is that the people there were leaders in a movement that worked *with* the planet rather than abusing it. People came from all over the world to find out and learn from their experiment. After a few hours of looking around, I set off to walk back to the bus stop.

The next day, back at the Tourist Information Centre, I browsed through the day tours. It always took me a lot of time to decide what to do. In the end, I took two day trips out of Inverness, which I enjoyed a lot, especially the one to Loch Ness. As we went up the loch by boat, it was quite rough, with waves breaking over the bow. I definitely didn't see "Nessie."

When we left the boat, I walked around the ruins of Urquhart Castle, ending up at the ubiquitous tourist shop. I heard one of the assistants commenting about it being so hot, that it was a heat wave. The temperature was 22 degrees Celsius; I couldn't believe it! I couldn't help saying that they had obviously not been to Australia, where a heat wave starts at about 40 degrees and lasts more than a week.

I usually get a fridge magnet from most places that I visit. I have so many it's a wonder the fridge works! But I get a lot of pleasure looking at them, even now. I went through the museum and other guided activities, and then I did the return trip to Inverness by boat, back down Loch Ness. The weather that time was not quite so kind—misty and grey. Still, I was looking forward to another outing with improved weather the following day.

That next outing was the Jacobean tour. This one interested me a lot, mainly because when I had my first reading after I returning home from my first trip, one of the first things the psychic reader asked was, "Were you a Jacobean?" I had no idea what she was talking about, as I'd never studied history at all, but now it suddenly made sense.

I really enjoyed these tours; there was so much to learn, and I felt I was a real beginner.

I visited a few shops and bought myself a kilt and some warm boots, for the weather had turned much cooler by then. I also went to the Guy Fawkes night at a big park. It took me about an hour to walk around the path that I was told to take. This path circled the huge park, and since it was so dark, I was getting a bit nervous. Eventually, though, I got there. When they lit the fire, the heat was incredible. Although we were thirty metres away behind a fence, we could still feel its intensity. There was a huge crowd, and the bagpipes were playing. At the end of the night, and not quite knowing my way home, I followed the crowd and ended up in town.

I would call Inverness my spiritual home, as I felt like I belonged there—and I still do. There was so much to love, the pretty bridges over the water, the churches, Loch Ness, and so much more. That week went fast. I think I could have stayed longer and filled the time if I'd had it. I loved the area and all the exploring I did.

Back in Edinburgh

Soon enough, it was time to go back to Edinburgh. When I returned, I joined the Red Bus tours to ensure that I saw as much of the place as possible. First, I travelled to the Palace of Holyroodhouse (also known as Holyrood Palace). We have nothing like that in Australia, and it was a real eye-opener with all its wealth and grandeur.

Another thing I wanted to see was the queen's ship, the royal yacht *Britannia*. I found the right bus, and when I arrived I had the added bonus of a big shopping centre right where the ship was tied up. The ship was quite interesting and gave us a chance to see how the other half lives. Women, by nature, can usually find lots to do in a shopping centre, so I spent hours in there as well. By that time, I only had three days until my return to Australia. Given that the weather was getting quite cold, I was looking forward to the Australian sunshine again.

James and I were walking down the street when suddenly I got a flash of a vision. It was of Dave, my friend back home who was suffering from cancer. In the vision, his face appeared emaciated. I wondered if that meant he had passed over, and I mentioned it to James. I had no way of checking at that time, so I just made a note of it in my dream book as usual.

Then James surprised me by saying, "You never got that massage, did you?" I said that I didn't. So he suggested that maybe he could do it for me. Now he tells me! We went to James's place, and I had the best massage I'd ever had. It did a lot for me.

Maybe James didn't realise it, but he did a lot to restore my faith in men, and he certainly boosted my confidence. My trip that time around was much better in so many ways. I was actually going home happy!

On a really freezing cold morning, James took me to the station to catch the train back to London. After our goodbyes, I was on my way, and I actually enjoyed the trip back. I only had one day in London and then it was off to the airport. I took advantage of having a long bath in the hotel; it was a real luxury to just soak away the tension of the past year.

On my return journey, the plane was half empty, giving me all the seats on the window side to myself. I could stretch out and have a good sleep, a more rested sleep, than I'd had in a long time.

After a short break in Kuala Lumpur, we were on our way again. Once more I had plenty of room—but after a good rest on the first leg, I didn't really need more sleep.

It was a long trip, and it was good to be back home in the warmth of Australia. I landed in Sydney, and my son met me at the airport. We drove to his place in Newcastle.

I had ordered a new car just before I left for my trip, and I still had a wait before it arrived from Japan. The big day came two days before Christmas, and at last I had my own transport again. It was a nice new Toyota Corolla, which I drove all the way back home.

When I returned to Diane's place, I noticed that she had netting all around the front door. I thought it was to keep the cats from scratching at the door to be let in, but no—it was to keep the snakes out! That put me on edge a bit. A few days later, she called out to my end of the house to come and have a look, and sure enough, a brown snake, one of Australia's deadliest, was caught in the netting. That was the end for me. I told her I would be moving back to town!

After viewing a few places, I found the perfect place close to town. As happened with my previous flat, the right one presented itself at the right time. I applied and successfully rented it without delay. It was close enough to walk into town if I didn't want to use the car, and it had a garden that I could restore.

The next time I went to Diane's house, she had some visitors there whom I knew. They were quite amazed at how much better I looked compared to when I'd returned from my previous journey. I actually felt normal again.

One of the first things I had to do was visit Dave, but alas, he had died. I asked about when it was that he had passed; given the time difference between the two countries, I determined it was exactly the time when I had received my vision about him.

Other Lives and Their Remembrances

Today, there are so many true stories of young children remembering their former lives. Children who have not had time to be filled with the ways of the world, and yet their remembrances have been verified as correct in many instances.

I can understand why we are not supposed to remember too much of a former life. Like a school exam, if we knew all the answers before the test, there would be no point in taking it. If we knew what we had come to achieve beforehand in this life, I suggest that we wouldn't bother trying and consequently would learn nothing of value. From my experience in Scotland, I understand that the emotional pain associated with foreknowledge can be devastating.

The one thing I'm glad about is that at least I was at a mature stage of my life and had some spiritual knowledge under my belt when I experienced the visions and the reliving of former experiences. Otherwise, I believe I would not have been strong enough to survive them. This surely was the biggest test I'd had yet.

The lesson that I believe was critical for me to learn in this lifetime was about suicide. I had taken my own life in the past, and it plagued me in this life. I learnt that this wasn't a solution to a problem. When things got too much in this present life, it appeared really easy to see suicide as the solution—a misguided way to escape the pain when no light is seen at the end of the tunnel. I had to learn the true value of life. I now know that if I took that sad option once more, I would just have to come back and learn that lesson all over again. I don't want that.

In my meditation and dreams, I've seen a life in Egypt. I've also clearly seen, at another time, a life as a priestess or someone in a similar position in a church in Greece or Rome.

In one deep meditation, I saw Harry and myself high up in the Andes Mountains as two men with very brown creased skin, so I assumed we were quite old. I have always had an affinity with South America, although I've never been there. I love the music and the people, and I have wanted to go to Machu Picchu for a long time. The music elicits a special response in me, a sense of excitement and sensuality.

The Wash-Up

I've had much time to reflect on the hard lesson I had to learn, and it's taken me some years to get around to writing about it, despite three different clairvoyants or mediums in separate readings over the years all telling me that there would be a book. I didn't really feel I could do it, and I certainly didn't have the confidence.

In my last reading, I was told as soon as I walked into her room, before the reading had started, "You've been told about doing this book before, haven't you?" I smiled and confirmed that indeed I had been told twice before and had also been scolded for not having started to write. That time I listened and started writing and compiling this book.

I had long accepted that my story was a karmic event and wouldn't affect me during the course of doing the book, but after getting to the part of recalling the battle scenes, I started having dreams about them, and about Stephen, all over again. While sitting typing one day, my mind wandered to when I had to leave Stephen in London, and the tears welled up in my eyes. I had to mentally turn off the image before I could resume writing. Maybe I'll never get over it.

When I think back to this event in my life, I can hardly believe that this was me, so pathetic and out of control. If someone had offered me a million dollars to stop crying, I would not have been able to do it. It's still hard to believe.

Today, now that I'm with my Scottish man Jim, who comes from Glasgow, I feel much more settled and happy. It took some time for him to get used to me knowing things before he had a chance to tell me. I can recall one day when I had come in the door and he said he had to confess something to me. Immediately I said "you have eaten all that corn meat that was left over haven't you". He turned around and said "how could you know that" Sometimes it's hard to keep my mouth shut because it looks like I'm spying but really it's so automatic and quick, the words come out before I even have time to think.

I was surprised how the writing of this story affected me. The question has been asked of me, what would happen if I suddenly met up with Stephen again, what would I do? I can only hope it doesn't happen, because I don't know how I would handle it.

Today

My main aim now in this life is to help where I can and keep up with the meditation, card-making, jewellery-making, and healing. In between those things, I play lawn bowling three days a week and walk whenever I get spare time.

The last few years, I've had many more medium experiences. I love this sort of work, and now that I have the book finished, I can get more involved in it. There is one goal I still have to achieve, and that is to have one or two acres of land which I can turn into gardens that are open to the public. I have devoted one big vision board to this particular dream. Over the years, I've seen how people flock to open gardens and how popular they are. I believe this is another form of silent healing.

When Amanda lost Robert, her husband, she was inconsolable. She had been with him her whole life. She knew his time was coming, but like everyone she wasn't really prepared for the event. On one of my bad days, when I was upset again, she said, "Alison, you are grieving." I felt she had hit the nail on the head, because that's just what it felt like. It was a loss, and she understood that.

I was sitting on my lounge room floor a few months after Robert had passed when I decided to concentrate on Amanda. I got nothing, so I turned my attention to Robert. Immediately, I got a picture of Robert and his friend the monk, whom I'd seen before in a meditation. They had their arms around each other's shoulders, like brothers.

I rang Amanda straight away and told her. She asked me if I remembered the song they had played at Robert's funeral. I didn't recall. She told me that his favourite tune was "Brothers in Arms," and, of course, that's just how I had seen them.

I've had many other visions and, using that gift, helped others whenever possible. It is what I really want to do in this life, so I will try my best.

Dreams, Visions, and Intuition

From the time I arrived back from the first trip, I had constant dreams about Stephen. Those dreams recurred for years—right up to when I was writing this book. Sometimes he would end up with me, which was a precious time, but often in the dreams I would begin with him and then he would go somewhere else. I could never find my way back to join him. This always caused me much anxiety, making me glad to return to the present, albeit in tears.

All my life, dreams have played an important role. I would dream every night, and sometimes I would wake up feeling like I'd been extremely active all night because I felt so tired. So many times I used to ask God to please let me have a break from the dreams for just one night. "Please, a break before the next wave hits me." I didn't get any respite; I would still dream every night. But overall, in hindsight, the dreams have been very helpful and useful, guiding me in times of extreme stress. Many times they were helpful for my sister, my daughter, and my friends. On balance, they have been more beneficial than burdensome.

One thing I have to accept is that my brothers and sister do not accept my record of what has happened to me. Even though I recorded so much evidence in my dream journal as proof, it has been hard for them to accept. But I cannot change what happened just to make others feel more comfortable.

My mother did believe me. In the last few years of her life, when I went to visit her, she knew that her time was coming and wanted to hear my views about the afterlife. We spent many hours discussing the subject. In the end, she said she felt much better about it, because in her growing-up years she was preached a religion of fire and brimstone—you were judged by a vengeful God as soon as you passed over.

The mainstream view is that we are asked to look back over our life just finished and see for ourselves how we think we have done, and whether we have achieved what we set out to do. We are given much help to understand where we might have gone wrong or where we did really well. We are not forced into anything. If we wish to do nothing, then we do nothing. Eventually, however, we would want to do something useful with our soul. Only the souls who have been a menace to the earth's people get no say about incarnating again so soon. I believe that the universal law would not allow them to return so quickly to cause destruction.

It follows, if I am correct, that it would take a long time for those like Hitler and other such people to really understand the consequences of their behaviour and to admit to what they have done before travelling the long road to rehabilitation. As there are no time constraints in the world of Spirit, there are no set limits for this. Only we, here on earth, set times.

So when my mother died, I felt a sense of peace for her. She had been in a great deal of pain, and I was glad she was free from it at last. When my dad died, it was much more of a struggle for me, but again, I accepted it, and sometimes I could feel when he was around. I finally had a dream of meeting up with him where I was crying with happiness. I woke myself up with tears coursing down my cheeks.

Dreams can be really weird and make no sense at all. Other times, they can be prophetic, which is very helpful in guiding us. Then again, dreams can also be symbolic, and in those instances it usually was quite easy for me to understand what they meant.

Prophetic Dreams

Here are some examples of prophetic dreams that were very helpful in times of stress:

- One night when I was about four months pregnant, I saw the baby in a bassinette beside my bed, and it was a girl. The next day I went out and bought pink clothes. There were those who doubted what I claimed to have seen. But it turned out that I did give birth to a girl. My mother had all boys for her grandchildren, and she desperately wanted to make something pink. She got her wish, even though she was too scared to believe me when I told her it would be a girl. When my baby was about four months old, she looked the way I had seen her in my dream.

- In another dream, I saw two planes collide in mid-air. At breakfast, I mentioned it to my husband. About five minutes later on the radio, we heard that this indeed had happened. I felt terrible, as there was nothing I could do about it. I've had many dreams over the years of planes crashing. My friend Lizzie sometimes has the same dream, but we don't know why.

- Another dream was of one of my children having twins. When my son rang one night to tell me his wife was pregnant, I told him, "One of you is going to have twins," meaning either him or my daughter. It wasn't long before he rang me to say they were having twins, and I was able to remind him of my dream.

- I awoke one morning knowing we were going to look at a house to buy. When we got there, the house was the same one I'd dreamt about the night before. The only difference was that the fireplace was not in quite the same place as in the dream, but there was a fireplace. This was the one we bought. Also, regarding the loan for the house, I had seen a loan advertised three times, so I took it as a sign that I was meant to go to that lender. We did and got the exact amount we needed. A lot of things seem to happen in threes for me.

- One morning I woke up feeling concerned about a dream I'd just had. It was as if there had been an earthquake. Everything was all topsy-turvy and confusing. A few hours later, I got a call from my sister telling me our mum had died in the early hours of the morning. My day certainly went topsy-turvy after hearing that news.

- In one particular dream, I was in a hospital in a lift trying to find a specialist's office. Later the next day, I was referred to a specialist surgeon. And it was in a hospital on the second floor, just as the dream had shown me.

- I was pregnant with my second child and at about the eight-week stage, and I'd had a few headaches. I felt that something was wrong, and so I went to see my doctor. I couldn't shake the feeling and mentioned it to the doctor. He said that there was nothing I could do about it anyway, even if there was something wrong. There was no such thing as an ultrasound in those days. All through the pregnancy I worried. When the baby was born, he was born with a problem with his right arm not being formed properly.

- Two years before my dad died, I dreamt of his passing. This was most unexpected, because my mother was definitely the more unwell of the two. But after that dream, I told my sister that Dad was going to go first. I dated this dream, and it was almost two years later that it happened this way. It was probably best for him, as he was going blind and he wouldn't have coped by himself.

Symbolic Dreams

These dreams are different from prophetic dreams in that they often show you what is occurring, rather than what's going to occur.

- In one dream, I was holding my beautiful baby. I was with many other mothers carrying their babies, and we were waiting for our husbands. They were all arriving from somewhere by bus. Then they got off the bus. However, my partner didn't arrive; he didn't get off. I interpreted this as showing me that although I'd been given a beautiful gift in my daughter, my partner and I were not staying together and would be going our separate ways. This is eventually what happened—precisely as I had interpreted.

- Another dream of the same type was one where I was in my grandmother's garden. On the borderline of the property, I looked over the edge and saw that the rocks were falling down a slippery slope and were very unstable. My partner ventured down the slippery slope. I looked and decided it was too dangerous to follow him, so I turned back. I then decided to weed the garden of the few remaining weeds. I found a strong sapling and I was going to pull it out, but then I saw new growth and decided to keep it. This clearly showed me that I would not follow his path anymore. The strong sapling was the new growth for me, meaning that I would be strong on my own—and I was.

- In another dream, I was being shown a gold medal, like an Olympic medal, and it was very close. I was looking at it and thinking I *could* do it. I looked down at my feet to see that I had joggers on and my legs were very powerful, like a man's legs. I knew I could do it. I interpreted this to mean that I was going to be strong enough to achieve the things I wanted.

- I had another dream where I saw myself from behind. I was standing up tall with my arms stretched out, and suddenly, I saw all these chains bursting off me and I was free, and there was sunshine all around. This one was easy to interpret—I was being freed of all the past problems and was ready to face a better, sunlit future.

- A good friend, a single mother with three children, was worried about a dream in which all her teeth fell out. Knowing her situation, I said to her, "If you lost all your teeth, you would feel that you couldn't face anyone, and you'd feel like people would think the worst of you." In this dream, she was worried that the children (the teeth) would want to go and live with their father, and if that happened people would think she was a failure as mother. This wasn't the case, as she was doing the best she could under difficult conditions. They had a right to go to their father, but I knew that the situation would not work out, so I urged her, "Don't worry about that." She got what I was saying, but there was complete silence from all the others in the family who were listening while they were sitting at the table. Then my cousin just said, "Wow."

Visions

Visions are common for a lot of people, but most don't take them seriously enough. If I asked a person to imagine a setting that was paradise, most people would see a tropical island, or something that they would easily love. These are what we call *imaginings*. Visions are pictures that come to you automatically, unaided. Sometimes there is nothing you can do about them, and you wonder why you are sent these images. Other times you can actually help someone by understanding what you have seen.

Here is an example of this: I was at my daughter's place for lunch on Mother's Day. All of a sudden, I started to get a warning about someone I knew; she had a problem with her car, and I needed to call her. I told her I didn't know what she was doing, whether it was that she was driving too fast or not concentrating on her driving, but she had to slow down. From there on, it's all you can do. Some months later she told me she'd had trouble with her wheels and subsequently had to get them fixed. There have been many others visions that are personal to family members and which, out of respect, I can't speak of.

Intuition

Most people have had a gut feeling about something being wrong. It's a warning, something we should listen to. If nothing comes of it, there's no harm done, but if there's something we can do, then we should look into it. Many women have that gut feeling of something being wrong with one of their children, or with their parents, and it's very unsettling until they find out why they have the feeling.

- One night, when in bed, I started to get butterflies in my stomach. I knew this meant that some profound event was imminent, but as usual, I didn't know what. I went to sleep feeling uneasy. At about 2:30 a.m., there was a knock on the front door. My friend was there with her children wanting shelter, as her husband was threatening them with a gun. Of course, we took them in and somehow got settled for the rest of the night, while she went back to try to reason with him.

- One day, at my house, another friend came to see us. She had breast cancer, and I asked her how it was going. She replied that she was doing really well and asked me to look at her, as she wanted some confirmation. Instantly, I knew that she wasn't going to make it. All I could do was give her moral support. She died some months later. Even though we might see the truth, there is nothing we can do about it. We will each make our transition when our time is up and not before.

- One of the unusual dreams I have is where I might want to wake up and think about it what I've seen in the dream space. Then I will go back into the dream to continue. If this can be achieved, it is quite handy, especially when the dream is particularly worthwhile and I want to get the most out of the experience.

- Sometimes I am conscious of being a totally free spirit and out of my body. In this state, I can fly anywhere. The feeling is unbelievable. The sense of freedom and love is all-consuming. There are no words to explain the feelings in the non-physical state. I only have to think it, and the next moment I am flying. Many times people are watching me and wondering how I'm flying, but even though I show them, they can't seem to achieve free flight. I never want this dream to end. The trouble is that it only happens every few years.

- I was doing job training with several other people who were attending a course. One morning, after many days of sending out resumes, I heard the phone ring. I felt a feeling go through me, and I said, "That call is for me." I just knew. They all looked at me questioningly, but sure enough it was, and the caller was asking me to go for an interview. Twice more over the following days, the same thing happened. The others couldn't understand how I knew, but I was right each time. Being a super-sensitive person means just that. The initialism *ESP* stands for *extrasensory perception*. Just as a dog can hear sounds beyond the human ear, so can people who are psychic. They can tune in better than most people to another level. I believe it's something we are born with, but it can be developed like any other skill if we are willing to put the work in through meditation. In many cases, it comes naturally—but when I was young, I didn't have much knowledge about it, and I certainly had no confidence to believe in myself to use it.

- One day, while I was driving home to Brisbane, I started to feel very teary and sad. I started to wonder what on earth was wrong with me. I couldn't shake it. This went on for hours. I examined my mind to see if it was my mum at the source of my emotion, but I got no feelings there. Next day, I rang Amanda, and she told me that her dog had died and that she was very upset, so I knew that's what I had been picking up.

- Another day I felt terrible pain, suffering, and hopelessness. After a few hours, I rang my sister to see if she was okay, but she said she was fine. This feeling continued all day, and it really bothered me. The next day I rang her again, but this time she said it was our mum, who'd had enough and wanted to "leave the planet." I understood what Mum was feeling. It's so hard to watch and feel someone suffer like that knowing you can't help.

- One morning when I woke up, I felt an urge to ring my friend on the Sunshine Coast about reiki. I did so and asked if I could come up, as I had a strong feeling about being there. She told me I couldn't have picked a better day, as her son's friend was a reiki master and would be there all day. I ended up staying the night and had great discussions with this man on many things. Being sensitive for me means I can feel quite high after picking up on happiness or love, but if I pick up on someone or something that is really negative or sad, then it affects me considerably, and I can feel pain associated with that person or situation.

Although we are told we have a free will, I believe that our free will is within the confines of the lessons we've returned here to learn. I decided when I was about twenty-two years of age that there was no one to help me at that the lowest point of my life, and I would just have to work through it on my own. There are, I believe, no accidental occurrences and no coincidences.

An interesting thing happened when I was not at church on one particular day. The next day my friend called and said that a visiting clairvoyant from Brisbane had asked for anyone in the congregation by the name of Alison. My name is not a common name in our church, so my friend piped up and said that she knew someone of that name. He gave her his phone number and told her to tell me to ring him. Of course I did, and he told me he got my name in meditation. He decided to make enquiries, even though he gets many names during meditation. He felt this was different. He was guided to give me a reading and to not charge me for it. So I drove to his place and had the reading. He told me of a warning and other things of great interest to me at the time.

Last year Jim and I decided to go up the coast to the trendy beach of Noosa a few hours north of Brisbane. A really popular and beautiful beach but we wanted to go to the shady side where the water came into an inlet, nice and calm. We both set up our chairs and got our books out to read. I started to hear a voice calling out a name in my head. At first I ignored it but it kept happening. As I didn't know anyone by this name, I asked Jim if he knew anyone with this name. He said yes but why.

Then it dawned on me that this was someone he knew that wanted to pass on a message.

He kept saying "I was sick you know" Jim confirmed that. From there on I just talked straight to Jim as the messages came. "He's saying that he liked you" This surprised Jim a bit. I then asked this man to provide some proof and asked how many children he had. The answer came back as three, so asked Jim if this was right. Yes, this was true, but I kept going by saying there was a problem with one of the sons, that there was some sort of disagreement between the father and son. I asked Jim what this was about. He told me of the circumstance behind this. This probably went on for about ten minutes surprising Jim no end.

Next day another name came to me out of the blue. Again I asked Jim did he know of this man and if he knew whether he had passed over. He knew who I was talking about but had not known if he had died as he hadn't seen him for quite a number of years.

Then about July I asked Jim if his sister was strong enough to face some problems I saw coming up. He asked me why. I said "because she and you are going to lose your mum, and then his sister would lose her husband as well. Jim found this a bit hard to believe but sure enough a few months later his mum passed then about six months later, his brother in law also passed.

It's hard sometimes but there are occasions where you have time to prepare and do and say the things you want to those people before they cross over. Don't take so many things for granted as we never are sure when we will not have our loved ones with us.

A few years before my mum and dad died, I wrote a letter to them outlining that whatever had happened in my life I had no regrets. That there was no blame as I took responsibility for my own battles to get through. I did not want to be one of those people who never told them I loved them, and then it was too late to do so after they had passed. My mum said that letter was one to frame, she really valued it and I'm glad I did because I was not with either of them when they passed.

Love and Learn

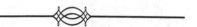

When we board a plane, we are given safety instructions: how to put our breathing masks on first before helping someone else, and the same with life jackets. This principle applies in life. We fix ourselves first. In this busy world, we need to take time out for ourselves and make our lives as meaningful as possible. I know that it is hard in this world, as it is at the moment. It seems to be in such a mess, but when we get our own life in order, we are in a position to help others. There is such a lack of love in the world; however, many people are praying for world peace and help. We must experience and know love before we can give it to others. If we can achieve this in one life, then we have gained a lot in the huge lesson on life and humanity.

Remember that what we do in this life will have consequences after we pass over. We should think thoroughly before we act. It is just as easy to do good as it is to do the wrong thing. By doing good, I believe we will save ourselves a lot of negative karma.

I would like to add something about revenge. Most people at some stage or other in their life believe that someone has hurt them and have felt the urge to get their revenge. Although this is an entirely human emotion, it is a total waste of time. It doesn't make us feel good. It doesn't satisfy the emotions. It does nothing at all except bring us down to the level of those who are doing the hurting. Most of all, we will have to pay for our vengeful thinking at some time. Short-term gain will have long-term pain.

We cannot change what might have happened, but we can decide not to go down the same track. We might think we can fool others, but deep inside, we know when we are doing the wrong thing. We cannot reverse mistakes, but we can do better if we think before acting.

I learnt the hard way that two wrongs don't make a right, and I believe that once we understand why we chose a particular action, we can choose a better response. Then again, that's why we are here: to learn. If we were all perfect, we wouldn't need to come to this earth to learn. For me, there is no person who is perfect. We are all a work in progress.

Many people know of someone with a terminal illness who has experienced a remission, or even an out-of-body experience following a serious accident. When that happens, we often find that people experiencing those extraordinary events change their lives dramatically. They have often seen or known that they must make a permanent change. Most then really appreciate life and want to do something to help others, to make a difference for the future of man and the planet. They realise that they have been given a second chance for a reason and must do whatever they can to make the remainder of their time worthwhile and meaningful. It's a big wake-up call.

So whatever the path you are on now, be kind to yourself and it will be easier to be kind to others. We cannot change what we've done in the past, but we can certainly do better once we've learnt the lesson—if we have a mind to learn.

I wish you all the best on your own journey.

Spiritual Poetry to Ponder

SOUL LOVE

The untold power of the sun above
Cannot be compared to the power of love.
However this force touches us here,
The opposite of love is fear.
All of us in our own special way
Have felt one of these from day to day.
How do you define affairs of the heart
Whether it's full or breaking apart?
It's something that cannot ever be measured;
It's one of those things that must be treasured.
When with your twin soul it's there to share,
Through life after life, the love stays there.
I can't explain it, but I *know* how it feels
When God touches us with his special seal.
There are no words, what can you say?
I just give thanks and continue to pray.
A soul love is true heaven on earth.
It's the true meaning of what we're worth.
Our past, the present, and our future are bright.
We'll walk together towards the light.
No limits, no boundaries, just aim for the best,
Then let it go and let God do the rest.

WINGS

The invisible wings by which we fly
From the deepest depths to the highest high
Love from the heart goes beyond the all
As it radiates to all no matter how small.
Time and distance no longer exist
Like love with your soul mate when you kiss.
You cannot comprehend when your heart sings
The pure magic that this love brings.
There is nothing else that you can say,
You just want to live like this each day.
Life becomes such a beautiful game
Because of such joy and sometimes pain.
So let's try to be free, let the love come,
And know how it feels when we all become one.

A PRAYER

It's taken a while for me to see
That angels have always been with me.
At times I know I've made a wrong choice,
But they always remind me with a clear strong voice.
More and more I hear what they say;
I'm constantly amazed as I go through each day,
Where I once seemed to feel on my own,
Now I know I'm never alone.
I'll take whatever help they give
And now I love the way I live.
I'm comfortable with the way I am,
Following my path the best I can.
So thank you angels for coming to me
To help me realise I can be me.
My thanks to God for this I pray
That he walks with me as I face each day.

THE EARTH

I am made of beauty for all to see
From the height of the sky to the deepest sea.
See with your eyes and use with pleasure
All that is here, but take good measure.
There may be not much left if you keep going this way,
So stop the abuse and learn each day—
Learn to restore all the harm you've done
For I am the earth when it's all said and done.

WHEN ONE LEAVES

A life together is better than gold.

One now is gone and the other grows old.

How do you fill that empty space

When life goes by at such a pace?

It's the loneliest journey that one can take.

Some call it life, others say fate.

The two hearts are still ongoing as one today

For the one who is gone and the one who stays.

Our need to touch again cannot be met;

We'd give our all, but no, not yet.

Reunion when it comes is worth the wait.

You know when time comes, he'll be first at the gate.

You know he feels the same as you,

But he also knows you have work to do.

So hang in there, the time will come

When you're both together again as one.

TEARS

Have you ever really thought about tears?
Some from happiness, some from fears,
The mysterious thing that causes the flow
I'd really like to know why it is so.
You shed so many, but the well's still there.
Is it telling you that you still do care?
Emotions and feelings flow from the soul
Whether you're young or just getting old.
Sometimes the pain seems too much to bear
You feel alone with no one to care.
We must go on and never give in,
To find somehow our strength from within.

REFLECTIONS

I wake in the morning; it's not yet quite light.
We take it for granted that day follows night.
The sounds at this time are good to the ears.
The birds are all busy, but many don't hear.
The beautiful sunrise I see from my bed
Sends a blaze of colour all over my head.
Now I wonder one day what would happen to men
If all this beauty came to an end.
I feels so ashamed of the little I know;
It's all been put there to help us to grow.
There was a time when we cared for each other
But it's been lost in the world of Big Brother.
No more morals, respect, family, or honour—
We're all too busy working for the dollar.
We've learnt very little from our errors gone by.
It's never too late to give it a try.
Forget about self and give from the heart
To help someone else and just be a part
Of God's big family, which was built from love,
And always remember to give thanks up above.

TODAY

Look at our society, see how we live.
We're good at taking but have nothing to give.
Violence and greed are a way of life;
God help the family, man and the wife.
The kids are all ruined; they care only for self,
Their parents' values thrown on some shelf.
Sex is used as a tool to sell,
And if you don't like it you can go to hell.
There's no ambition, drive, or hope—
To escape this, they turn to dope.
There must be someone to blame this on;
Many blame God, but that is also wrong.
Man is to blame for this giant leap,
For what we have sown, we now must reap.

CHILDREN

The life of a child is easy to follow—
They always know there will be tomorrow,
They don't know of ifs, buts, and mights,
They always know that day follows night.
They don't need money when there's lots to do,
There's rainbows to ride in the sky so blue.
Mum's always there and Dad's around
Just in case they fall to the ground.
To be held and cuddled is all they need;
They know not of sorrow, hunger, and greed.
So let's take a lesson from their simple ways,
And learn how to live from day to day.

REACHING OUT

Sometimes our life is full of hard knocks.
There are times when we're sure we've hit the rocks
But look up, not down, for when you're that low
You can be sure there's nowhere to go.
So reach out, take hold with your teeth.
We must learn to walk on our own two feet.
Accept help from others who wish to be kind—
They may have been there, you're one of their kind.
They may be only a few steps ahead
But they won't desert you and leave you for dead.
We're all on one path, for there is no other.
The sooner we realise we're all sister and brother
The easier our climb upwards will be.
The nearer to him, we will surely see
That the heaven that's been promised from him,
We just have to knock and he'll let us in.

THE PENNY DROPS

The penny drops, the truth sinks in,
We are on the outside, what we think within
The possibilities like time and space,
It's all been there in front of our face.
In many ways, it's just a relief.
The simple truth is the word *belief*.
From this day forward, put your thoughts to the test—
No limits or boundaries, just ask for the best.
If, by example, we can be a light
To give to others this vision of sight,
Then the light itself can never go out,
So make it your business to spread it about.

THINKING

The time has come, so they say;
We all have to face this day.
As we look back and wonder why,
Why did I not just give it a try?
Way too scared by doubts and fears,
I didn't say much lest others should hear.
I learnt much but want so much more,
I need more time to even my score.
We know nothing when we are young and bright
With no experience, we have no insight.
Mistakes and lessons along the way,
Trying to make the best of each day,
We cannot undo our past no matter what
Time goes too fast, so give it your best shot.
We are all accountable at the end of the road;
Stop and let others share the load.
I believe there is goodness in everyone.
We need to choose and get the job done,
So let's choose better, then we can see
How much more beautiful this world can be.

❧ HELP ❧

The tunnel is dark, I see no light,
I'm tired of the struggle and don't want to fight.
There is help, but I cannot ask,
Just too tired to do this task.
A hand is out, is anyone there?
Let me see if anyone cares.
I know it's hard, but hang on tight,
It can be different as day is to night.
You can come back, just have the will;
We'll just say that you've been ill.
We have you now, you're safe in here,
You are precious and loved and have nothing to fear.
To learn again, you are so loved
And give thanks again to God above.

Printed in the United States
By Bookmasters